Carol Doak's *Simply Sensational* 9-Patch Stars

MIX & MATCH UNITS TO CREATE A GALAXY OF PAPER-PIECED STARS

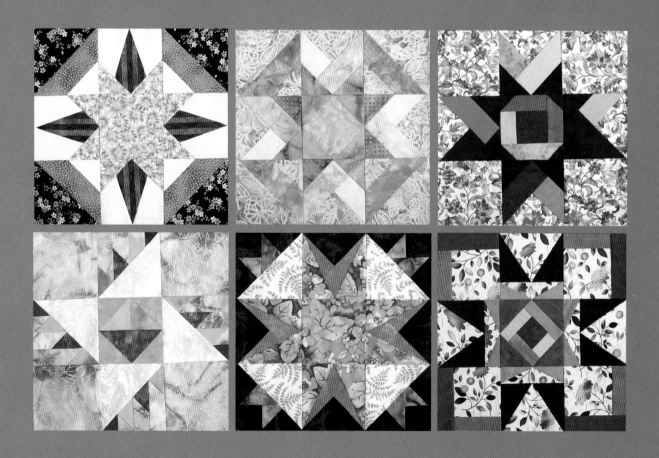

C&T PUBLISHING

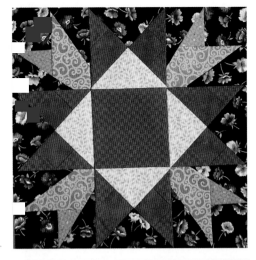

Text © 2005 Carol Doak
Artwork © 2005 C&T Publishing, Inc.

PUBLISHER: Amy Marson
EDITORIAL DIRECTOR: Gailen Runge
ACQUISITIONS EDITOR: Jan Grigsby
EDITOR: Liz Aneloski
TECHNICAL EDITORS: Carolyn Aune, Susan Nelson
COPYEDITOR/PROOFREADER: Wordfirm Inc.
COVER DESIGNER: Christina Jarumay
DESIGN DIRECTOR/BOOK DESIGNER: Rose Sheifer
ILLUSTRATOR: Mary Ann Tenorio
PRODUCTION ASSISTANTS: Matt Allen, Kiera Lofgreen
PHOTOGRAPHY: Luke Mulks, unless otherwise noted

Published by C&T Publishing, Inc., P.O. Box 1456, Lafayette, CA 94549

Library of Congress Cataloging-in-Publication Data
Doak, Carol.
  Carol Doak's simply sensational 9-patch stars : mix & match units to create a galaxy of paper-pieced stars / Carol Doak.
       p. cm.
  Includes bibliographical references and index.
  ISBN 1-57120-284-6 (paper trade : alk. paper)
  1. Patchwork--Patterns. 2. Quilting--Patterns. 3. Stars in art. I. Title: Simply sensational 9-patch stars. II. Title.

TT835.D59147 2005
746.46'041--dc22

Printed in China
10 9 8 7 6 5 4 3 2 1

Dedication

This book is dedicated to Sherry Reis, a star who shines as brightly today as she did more than 25 years ago when we discovered our special friendship in a quilting class.

Acknowledgments

My heartfelt thanks and appreciation are extended to
Timeless Treasures fabrics for the wonderful fabrics
used in many of the quilts and blocks,
Prym Dritz for the Omigrid rulers I love to use,
Bernina Sewing machines for their support,
Jim Salamon and Miriam Neuringer of Quilt-Pro Systems
for the Foundation Factory program to print the
foundations used in this book, Betty Oxley
and Becky Doane for their enthusiastic offers to
sew some of the star blocks, Kathryn Blais
for her beautiful and creative machine quilting,
Jan Grigsby and Amy Marson of C&T Publishing for
their excitement and support of this book, and Liz Aneloski
of C&T Publishing for being my guide as we brought
Carol Doak's Simply Sensational 9-Patch Stars to life.

Table of Contents

Alabama, page 26

Alaska, page 26

Arizona, page 27

Arkansas, page 27

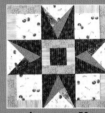
California, page 27

Colorado, page 27

Connecticut, page 28

Delaware, page 28

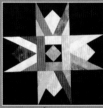
Florida, page 28

Georgia, page 28

Hawaii, page 29

Idaho, page 29

Illinois, page 29

Indiana, page 29

Iowa, page 30

Kansas, page 30

Kentucky, page 30

Louisiana, page 30

Maine, page 31

Maryland, page 31

Massachusetts, page 31

Michigan, page 31

Minnesota, page 32

Mississippi, page 32

Missouri, page 32

Montana, page 32

Nebraska, page 33

Nevada, page 33

New Hampshire, page 33

New Jersey, page 33

New Mexico, page 34

New York, page 34

North Carolina, page 34

North Dakota, page 34

Ohio, page 35

Oklahoma, page 35

Oregon, page 35

Pennsylvania, page 35

Rhode Island, page 36

South Carolina, page 36

South Dakota, page 36

Tennessee, page 36

Texas, page 37

Utah, page 37

Vermont, page 37

Virginia, page 37

Washington, page 38

West Virginia, page 38

Wisconsin, page 38

Wyoming, page 38

Introduction

*T*hese paper-pieced star blocks are simple to make, yet the results are sensational. Even if you have never paper pieced before or made a star block with perfect points, you will discover success using these paper-pieced units. It is no secret that I love the accuracy paper foundation piecing produces and I love star blocks. It was natural for me to explore the concept of creating 9-patch star blocks using paper-foundation piecing methods. However, even I am in awe of the thousands of 9-patch star blocks resulting from the idea of combining simple 9-patch units. The designs range from very simple star blocks, completed quickly and accurately, to more intricate ones produced perfectly every time. I am so excited to share with you these easy methods for creating 9-patch star blocks!

In the Creative 9-Patch Star Options chapter, I share with you how easy it is to combine these simple paper-pieced units to create thousands of star blocks.

In the Tools, Fabric, and Foundation Preparation chapter, I describe the tools I use to produce paper-pieced patchwork and share methods for cutting fabric pieces accurately and efficiently.

In the Paper Piecing Techniques chapter, my tried and true paper-piecing methods are described in a step-by-step format to ensure success.

In the 9-Patch Star Blocks chapter, there are fifty 9-patch star blocks, one dedicated to the quilters in each state. In my previous book, *50 Fabulous Paper-Pieced Stars*, I presented an eight-pointed star for each state. In this book I have created 50 more state blocks—9-patch stars this time. Each block references the units used to produce it.

The Quilt Projects chapter presents twelve exciting star quilts, ranging from 36" x 36" to 72" x 72", each with simple-to-follow instructions. The Quilt Finishing chapter covers how to finish your quilt.

In the Foundation Units and Cutting Lists chapter, you will find the 40 foundation units and their very important cutting lists.

The Resource chapter explains the installation of the wonderful, wonderful, wonderful Foundation Factory program that is included with this book. The Foundation Factory program will let you print the foundations for your star blocks from your computer printer. This is a very easy to-use program and one that you will love.

Now that I have described all that is included, please take some time to read through the book before you begin your first block. There are lots of tips and suggestions to ensure that your paper-pieced 9-patch star block experiences are efficient and enjoyable.

Creative 9-Patch Star Options

I can hardly wait to begin describing all your creative options when combining the paper-pieced units to create 9-patch star blocks, but I am going to start at the beginning and try to contain myself.

Foundations

The foundation drawing is the reverse side of the block. When the unit design is symmetrical (e.g., Unit 3), this is of no consequence because the finished unit design appears the same on both sides, although the number locations are reversed. However, when the block design is asymmetrical (e.g., Unit 8), the finished unit design is the reverse image of the foundation design.

Symmetrical unit design, Unit 3

Asymmetrical unit design, Unit 8

The unit foundations are presented in a 4" size, and the small images to the right show how the unit will appear as a finished unit and how this unit can be used in a 9-patch star block.

Unit 7

Unit 7

Star Points

I created foundations for the star points and combined the foundation star-point units with squares of fabric to produce 9-patch star blocks quickly and accurately.

Unit 1 Unit 1 combined with fabric squares

Center Units

Next, I created foundation units that could be used as paper-pieced star centers and added these units to the mix.

Unit 22 Unit 1 and Unit 22 combined with fabric squares

Corner Units

Finally, the corner foundation units were added, resulting in a stunning star block design.

Unit 37 Unit 1, Unit 22 and Unit 37 combined

Combining Units

Simple foundation units and fabric squares are combined to create 9-patch star blocks. There are twenty star-point unit designs, ten center unit designs, and ten corner unit designs, resulting in thousands of possibilities for star block designs made from simple unit combinations.

To illustrate the variety of creative options available, a star-point unit, a center unit, and a corner unit were combined to produce several star block designs.

| Unit 2 | Unit 26 | Unit 40 |
| Star Points | Centered Units | Cornered Units |

The following illustration shows the resulting twelve star blocks.

To illustrate this point even further, I selected eighteen point units, seven center units, and seven corner units and placed them in a chart format. Pages 9 to 11 show the star combinations produced by combining the eighteen star-point units and the seven center units. Pages 12 to 14 show the star combinations produced by combining the eighteen star-point units and the seven corner units. However, these 252 star block combinations are just the beginning, because many more star block combinations are possible when you combine the star-point units, the center units, and the corner units in each star block.

Selected Point Unit and Center Unit Combinations

Point Units

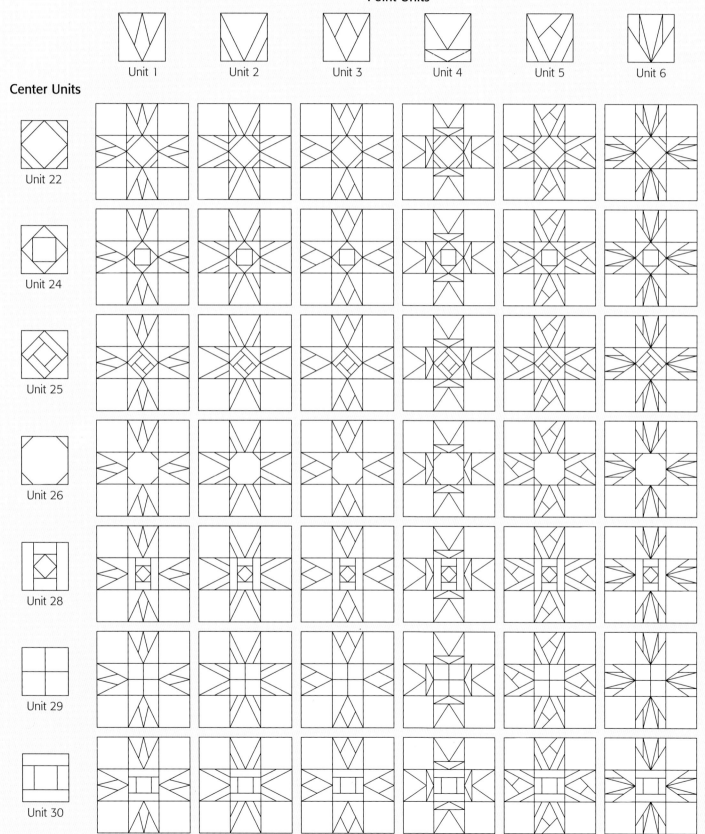

Unit 1 Unit 2 Unit 3 Unit 4 Unit 5 Unit 6

Center Units

Unit 22

Unit 24

Unit 25

Unit 26

Unit 28

Unit 29

Unit 30

Selected Point Unit and Center Unit Combinations

Point Units

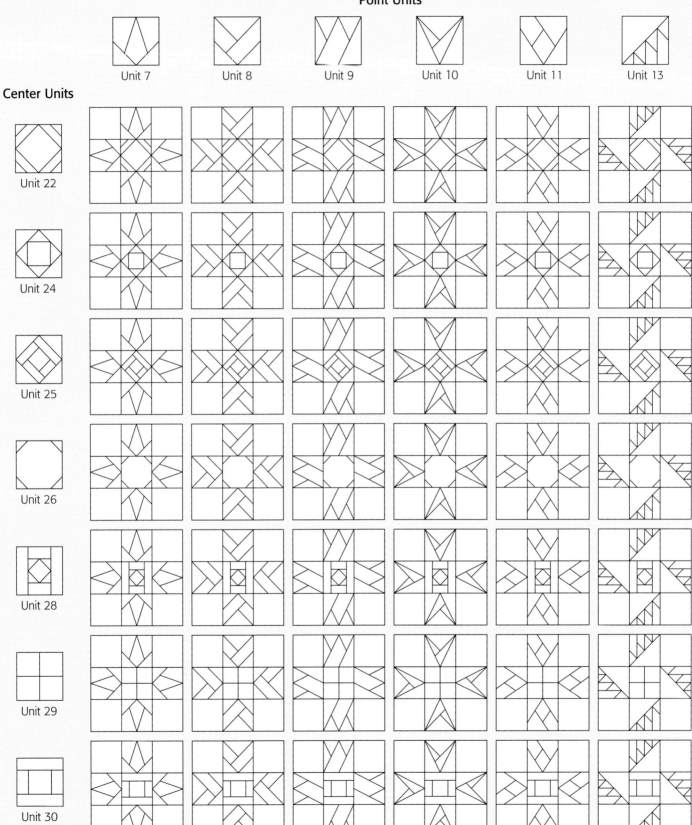

Unit 7   Unit 8   Unit 9   Unit 10   Unit 11   Unit 13

Center Units

Unit 22

Unit 24

Unit 25

Unit 26

Unit 28

Unit 29

Unit 30

Selected Point Unit and Center Unit Combinations

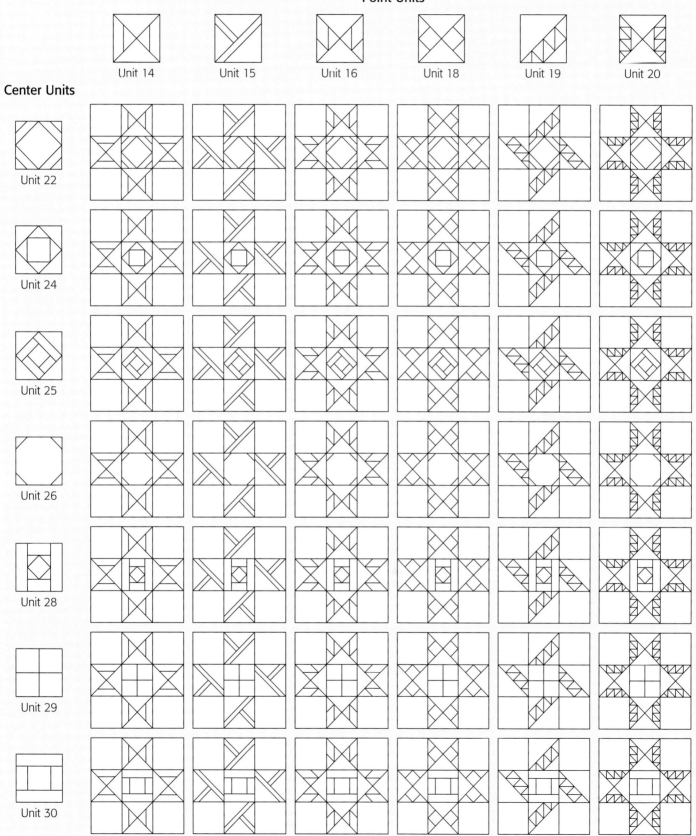

Selected Point Unit and Corner Unit Combinations

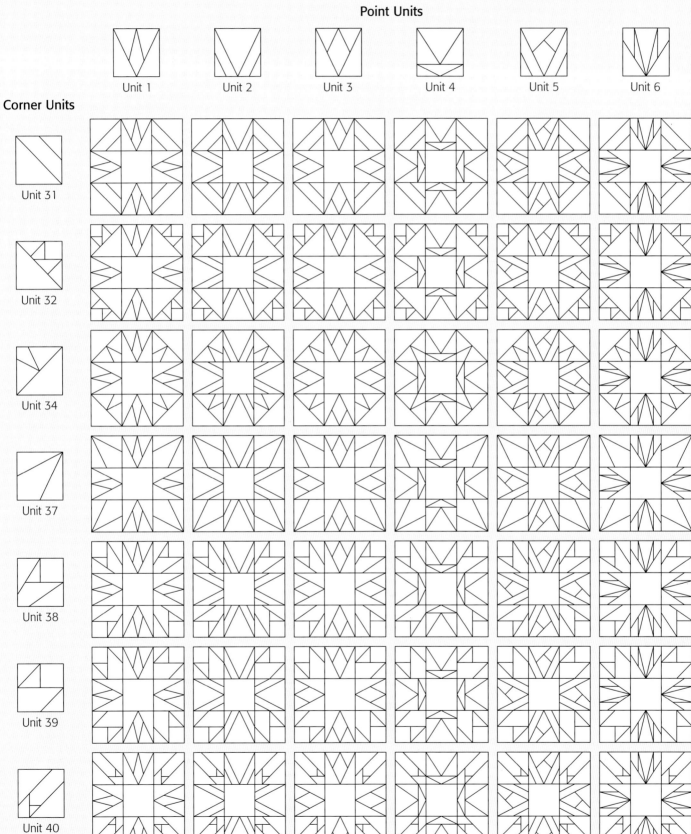

Selected Point Unit and Corner Unit Combinations

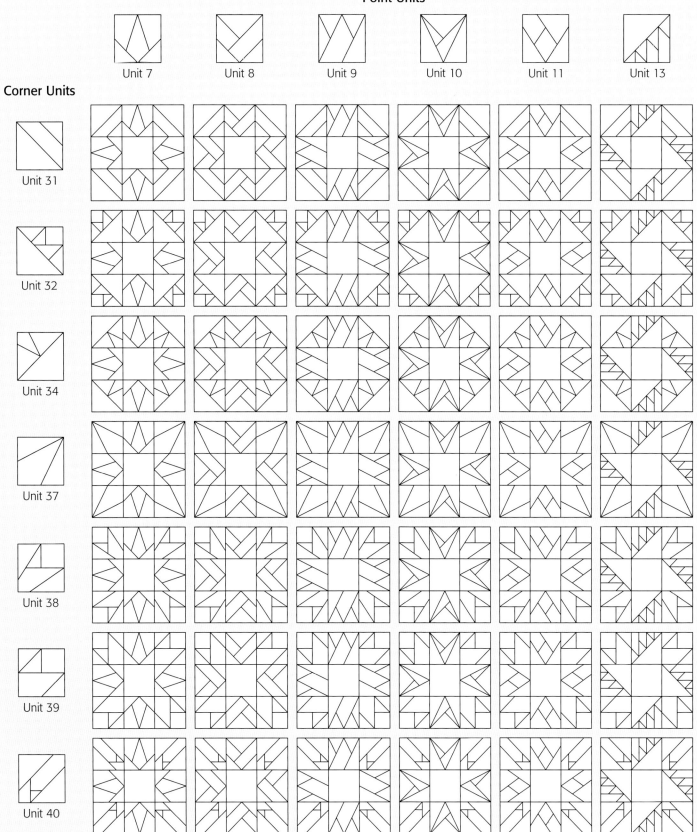

Selected Point Unit and Corner Unit Combinations

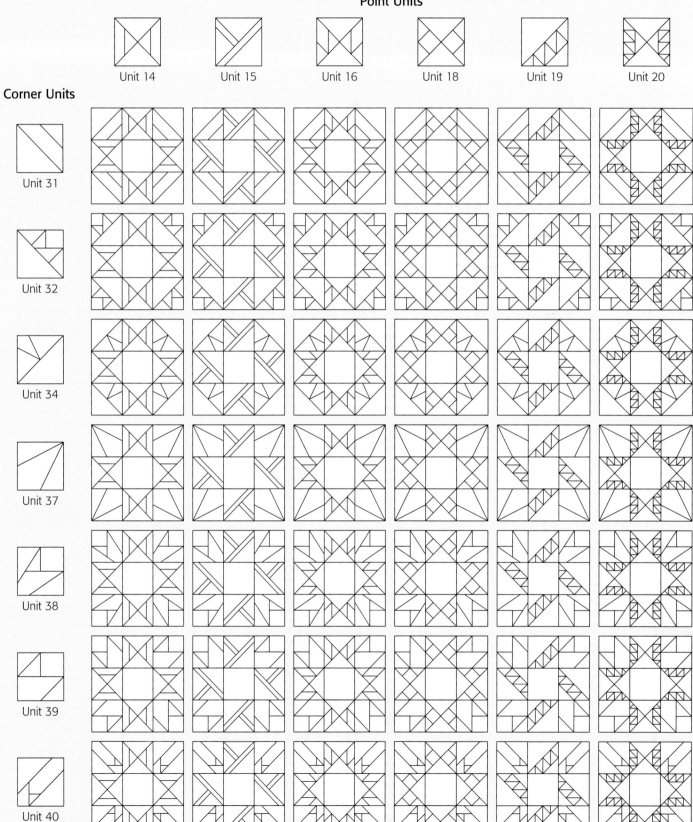

Point Units

Unit 14   Unit 15   Unit 16   Unit 18   Unit 19   Unit 20

Corner Units

Unit 31

Unit 32

Unit 34

Unit 37

Unit 38

Unit 39

Unit 40

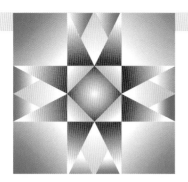

Tools, Fabric, and Foundation Preparation

Tools

Now that your creative juices are flowing, it is time to share with you the tools that make paper piecing easy and efficient.

Sewing machine—One in good working order equipped with a size 90/14 needle. The larger needle makes the paper easier to remove.

Open-toe presser foot—This foot will give you the best visibility while sewing.

Thread—I typically use white, gray, or black and only match thread color when joining blocks that are a solid color along the seamline.

Flat-head straight pins—Not only are these pins easier to handle, but the flat head will not get in your way when you fold the paper back along the edge of the postcard.

Rotary cutter and mat—I prefer the medium and large rotary cutters because they easily cut multiple fabric layers.

Rotary rulers—I have often claimed that I could be stranded on a deserted island with my 6″ x 6″ and 6″ x 12″ gridded rulers. I prefer rulers featuring yellow lines because it is easier to see that the yellow line is correctly placed on the foundation's black line. To ensure that the rulers do not slip on the paper, use the newer gripping rulers.

Add-A-Quarter ruler—This is one of those "must haves" to streamline your paper-piecing process (page 21).

Postcard—Use the edge of the postcard to fold the paper back on the next line you will sew. It just makes the folding step quick and easy (page 20).

Olfa rotary point cutter—If you need to remove a line of stitching, this wonderful tool will become your new best friend (page 22).

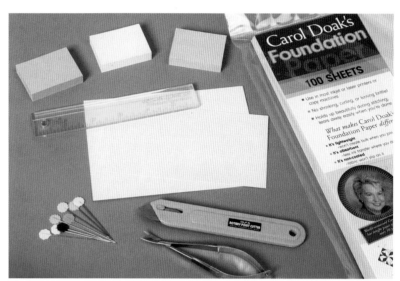

A few of the tools to make paper piecing easy

Scotch Brand removable tape—This tape will mend a torn stitching line and will provide a new foundation surface if you need to sew a line a second time. It is not as sticky as cellophane tape so it will not gum up your sewing machine needle (page 22).

Curved pointed snips—These snips permit you to cut your sewing threads on the top and bottom of the foundation at one time. They are a real time-saver (page 23)!

Staple and staple remover—Staple up to 9 sheets of foundations together and trim them all at one time (page 19).

Small stick-on notepads—Use these to label your precut fabric pieces with their location number(s) and unit.

Foundation piecing paper—I prefer to use lightweight newsprint paper because it is accepted by my computer printer and my copy machine, absorbs the ink, and holds up during the sewing process, yet it is flexible when joining units, does not produce bulk at seam intersections, and best of all, removes easily. Carol Doak's Foundation Paper is suggested (page 104).

Fabric and Foundation Preparation

As quilters, we have a love affair with our fabrics. The good news about paper-foundation piecing is that fabric grain placement is not important because the paper foundation supports the fabric to minimize stretching. However, fabric grain is important visually. Use nondirectional fabrics when the straight-grain edge of the same fabric will be placed at various angles on the foundation. In the first block example below, directional fabric is used in the background area of Unit 7 in the #2 and #3 locations, and the result is distracting. A nondirectional vine fabric is used in the second block example below and is a better choice for the #2 and #3 locations.

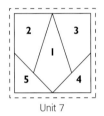  

Unit 7

Directional and nondirectional background fabric

Fabric can add detail to the foundation unit when a fabric element is centered in the #1 position. Trace the shape of the #1 position onto tracing paper and cut it out ⅜″ from the outside edge of the sewing line. Place the paper wrong side up on the right side of the fabric. Move it around the fabric to see opportunities to center an element. Once the element is isolated, cut it out along the edge of the paper. This takes a bit more time to cut the fabric pieces, but the detail is worth it. In the following example, a fabric element is centered in the #1 position of Unit 21.

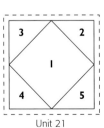  

Unit 21

Centering a fabric element to create detail

Cutting Fabric Efficiently

It is efficient to precut your fabric pieces prior to paper piecing, whether you are making one block or a quilt of many blocks. Each foundation unit has a cutting list that indicates the location numbers in the unit, the size to cut for the location(s), and how many pieces to cut for one star block. For Point Units 1 through 20 and Corner Units 31 through 40, the list indicates the number to cut for four units because you will make four points and/or four corners for each star block. For Center Units 21 through 30, the list indicates the number of pieces to cut for one unit because you will make one unit for each star block.

Before you cut the fabric pieces for your project, make a cutting list for your fabric placement. To illustrate the steps to follow in making your cutting list, Unit 2 (page 82) is used for one star block using the following red, white, and blue fabric placement. First, write your color choices on one foundation. Place the cutting list for Unit 2 alongside the foundation where the color choices are indicated. You will refer to this as you write up your personal cutting list.

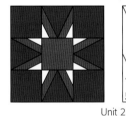 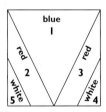

Unit 2

Cutting List for Unit 2

Location	Size to Cut	4 Units
1	4¾″ x 4¾″	4
2, 3	1½″ x 5½″	8
4, 5	1½″ x 3½″	8

Then, list your fabric choices and write the number to cut for one star block, the size to cut for the location number(s), and the location numbers where each fabric choice will be used. Be sure to include any plain fabric squares that will be used in the center or corners of the block. The plain fabric squares are always cut 4½" x 4½".

Personal Cutting List

Fabric	No. to Cut	Size to Cut	Location
Red	1	4½" x 4½"	Center square
	8	1½" x 5½"	2, 3
Blue	4	4¾" x 4¾"	1
	4	4½" x 4½"	Corner squares
White	8	1½" x 3½"	4, 5

In our example there is only one unit, but if you are using pieced corner units or a pieced center unit, then add a column after Location labeled "Unit" so you can designate the location numbers in the correct unit. Once the list is created, take a moment to arrange the items in the list for each fabric, with the larger cuts first, followed by the successively smaller cut sizes. Do this so you can cut a strip of fabric for the largest measurement and cut any smaller pieces from the remnants of the larger strip.

Gather your red, white, and blue fabrics; cut strips of fabric; subcut the strip(s) into the correct size of pieces; and label the fabric pieces in each cut group using small stick-on notes labeled with the location number of where they will be used. Write only the number on the note (and unit if you are using more than one unit). Do not write how many you cut or the size that you cut the pieces. You only needed that information for cutting purposes, and the fewer numbers on your notes, the better.

What if you are making a 25–star block quilt using this block? No problem. Simply multiply the number of pieces to cut for one block times 25 blocks to come up with the total number of pieces to cut for your quilt. Now you need to calculate how much fabric you will need.

Calculating Yardage

Step 1: Refer to the chart below to determine how many pieces can be cut from one fabric strip.

Cut Lengths	Number of Pieces Cut from 42" Strip
1"	42
1¼"	33
1½"	28
1¾"	24
2"	21
2¼"	18
2½"	16
2¾"	15
3"	14
3¼", 3½"	12
3¾"	11
4"	10
4¼", 4½"	9
4¾", 5", 5¼"	8
5½", 5¾", 6"	7
6¼", 6½", 6¾", 7"	6

Step 2: Divide the total number you need to cut by the number you can cut from one strip to determine how many strips to cut. In our star block example, 8 white pieces, each 1½" x 3½", were needed for one star block. To calculate the number of pieces needed for 25 star blocks, multiply 8 pieces times 25 blocks to determine that 200 pieces are needed. Looking at the chart, we see that we can cut 12 pieces, each 3½" long, from one strip. So in Step 2, divide the 200 pieces needed by the 12 pieces that can be cut from one strip to determine that 16.66 strips are needed; round up to 17 strips.

Number of pieces per block x number of blocks = total *pieces* needed

Example:
8 x 25 = 200 pieces needed

Number of pieces needed ÷ number of pieces in one strip = number of *strips* needed

Example:
200 ÷ 12 = 16.66 (round up to 17 strips needed)

Step 3: Multiply 17 strips times the width of each strip (1½″ in our example) to arrive at 25½″ of white fabric needed to cut the pieces to make 25 star blocks. Round up to the nearest yardage. We could round this up to 27″ (¾ yard), but that would leave only 1½″ of leeway for an oops, fabric shrinkage, and straightening the edge. I would purchase ⅞ yard or 1 yard of fabric. One can never have too much fabric!

Number of strips needed x width of each strip = amount of fabric needed in inches

Example:
17 x 1½″ = 25½″ (round up to nearest portion of a yard and add extra for mistakes)

Speed Cutting

Good news! I have calculated and provided the cut measurements for all the foundations! When cutting the fabric pieces to paper piece, you can speed up the process significantly by layering folded strips on top of each other. You can butt the long side of up to four stacks of strips together, and then crosscut through successive layered strips. The fabric pieces may shift slightly, but this is not a problem since the fabric pieces used in paper piecing do not have to be exact. In the following photo, 1½″ layered strips are crosscut at 4″ intervals. This is also an easy way to keep track of the number of pieces you have cut because you know how many pieces are in each stack.

Note: Do not use this technique when cutting 4½″ x 4½″ squares for the center and corner squares because you do want these to be as exact as possible. Cut these pieces from one folded fabric strip.

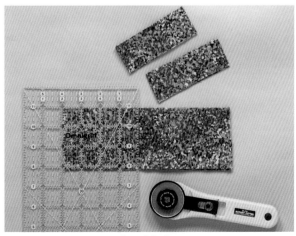
Speed Cutting

TIP

Place all the cut fabric pieces right side up in the stack. This truly will save you time and eliminate mistakes when paper piecing.

Measuring Fabric Sizes for Reduced or Enlarged Units

If you should decide to reduce or enlarge the foundation units to make a different star block size, you will need to calculate the correct fabric measurements. It is not a difficult task. First, print one copy of the new foundation size using the Foundation Factory program or use a photocopy machine to enlarge or reduce the foundation.

To measure the #1 piece, place the 6″ x 6″ rotary ruler over the #1 piece on the foundation in the same manner you intend to place the first fabric piece. Align the ¼″ line on the ruler with one seamline on the right and bottom. Looking through the ruler, determine the measurement that is ½″ beyond the furthest points of the two remaining seamlines. This will give you a fabric piece that is ¾″ larger than the area it needs to fill. Write this measurement on your foundation so you can use this information when creating your new cutting list. In the following photo, I have shaded in the #1 area so it is visible and placed the ruler on the foundation in this manner to determine that #1 should be cut 2¾″ x 4¾″.

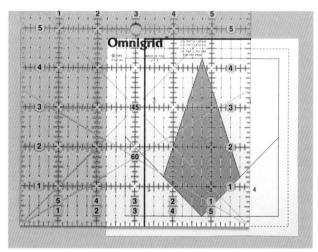
Measuring the #1 piece

To measure the subsequent rough cut fabric pieces, place the ¼" line on the ruler on the next seamline you will sew. Look through the ruler to determine ½" beyond the furthest part of the piece you are measuring. You may round up or round down to the nearest "fun line" on the ruler. I consider ¼", ½", ¾", and 1" the fun lines. In this case, the furthest part of the piece falls at 2⅛". Rather than cutting at 2⅝", I choose to round down to 2½". In the following photo, the #2 piece is measured at 2½" x 4".

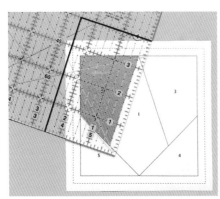

Measuring subsequent fabric pieces

To measure for half-square triangle pieces (straight grain on the short side of the triangle), measure the short side of the triangle and add 1¼" to this measurement. Cut a square this size and cut it once diagonally to produce 2 triangles. Mark a ◻ in the cutting list.

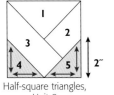

Half-square triangles, Unit 8   2" + 1¼" = 3¼"   2 half-square triangles

To measure for quarter-square triangle pieces (straight grain on the long side of the triangle), measure the long side of the triangle and add 1½" to this measurement. Cut a square this size and cut it in half twice diagonally to produce 4 triangles. Mark a ⊠ in the cutting list.

Quarter-square triangles, Unit 8   4" + 1½" = 5½"   4 quarter-square triangles

Once all the measurements are written on the foundation, create the new cutting list.

Paper Foundations

Photocopy Machines

Make photocopies from the original in the book and check your first copy against the original for accuracy. Do not make a copy of a copy because you will compound the slight distortions inherent in all photocopies. For a few dollars, the binding of this book can be cut off at a local print shop or office supply store and the book spiral bound to make it lie flat for easier photocopying. Use Carol Doak's Foundation Paper (C&T Publishing) for best results.

Foundation Factory Computer Program

I am so pleased that a Foundation Factory CD, permitting you to print accurate copies of the foundations in this book, is included with the book. This is a very easy-to-use program. Information about installing the CD is provided on page 102. The program lets you select the block that you would like to print, change the size, flip the block horizontally and vertically, print it shaded, and print multiples of the same block to a page, positioned with space between the blocks. There are some additional options that are clearly explained on the CD. I think you will love using it to print your foundations. But since I just invested in a paper shredder and was surprised to see prohibitive notices on the top of the machine indicating that you should not put your hand or your tie in the shredder, let me tell you what this CD will not do. It is not a quilt design program. You cannot change the fabric placement, create quilt designs, or calculate yardage, and there are no quilt designs on the program, only the unit foundations. The program will not create time to quilt. Well, maybe it actually will, because you will not be running out to make copies. But I know for a fact that it will not cook dinner for you.

Trimming the Foundations

Trim each foundation a generous ¼" beyond the dashed outside line (a generous ½" beyond the solid seamline).

TIP *Staple up to nine pages together in the center of each foundation unit and trim using a rotary cutter and rotary ruler. I have been using my rotary cutter to do this for more than ten years and have seen no excess dulling of my rotary blades.*

Paper-Piecing Techniques

You have arrived! The fabric pieces are cut and labeled. The foundations are made and trimmed. You are so ready to begin sewing!

Prepare the Sewing Machine

1. Place a size 90/14 needle in your machine. This needle will create a larger hole, making the paper easier to remove.

2. Place an open-toe presser foot on the machine. By open-toe, I mean that space in front of the needle is clearly visible so you can see that you are sewing on the line.

3. Set the stitch length to 18 to 20 stitches to the inch. On a machine that has a range of 0 to 5, this is approximately 1.5. If your stitch length is too big, it will be difficult to remove the paper. If it is too small, the paper will tear as you sew and accuracy will be lost.

Step-by-Step Paper Piecing

Before I describe the process for paper piecing, let me explain that the lined side of the foundation where the design is printed is the wrong side of the block and the blank side of the foundation is the right side of the block. Reverse thinking is required if you look at the lined side to determine fabric placement and turn the block over to place the fabric pieces on the blank side. I cannot think in reverse! I establish the lined side of the foundation as the mechanical side—the place where I will sew and take measurements. I establish the blank side as the visual side—the place where I will make visual decisions such as those relating to positioning fabric pieces correctly. You will be able to see through the paper when you hold it up to the light on your sewing machine. (In order to allow you to see through the foundations in the following photos, vellum paper foundations are used.)

1. Select the #1 fabric piece and place it right side up over the #1 area on the **blank side** of the foundation. Turn the foundation over to confirm that the fabric is extending at least ¼″ beyond all the #1 seamlines. Pin in place, parallel to the first seamline you will sew and away from the seamline. Use those wonderful flat-headed pins.

 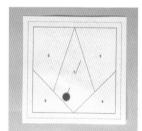

Place #1 fabric and pin.

2. With the lined side of the foundation facing up on the cutting mat, place a postcard on the line between pieces #1 and #2. (Plain card stock is used in the following photos so as not to be distracting.) Fold the paper over the edge of the card, exposing the excess fabric.

Place postcard and fold paper.

3. Place the Add-A-Quarter ruler on the fold and trim the exposed fabric ¼" from the fold using a rotary cutter.

Trim.

4. Place the #2 fabric right side up on the blank side of the paper over the #2 area approximating the position for piece #2. Flip the #2 fabric over and place it right sides together with the edge of the #1 piece just trimmed. Adjust the placement along this line so it will cover the #2 area when it is sewn and pressed open. Pin in place.

Place #2 fabric and pin.

5. Sew on the line between #1 and #2, extending the stitching about ½" at both ends.

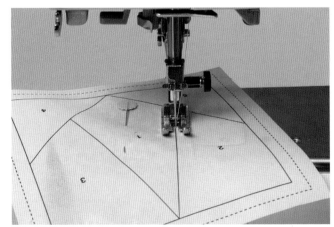

Sew.

6. Clip the threads and remove the pins. Press the #2 piece open with an iron on a cotton setting with no steam.

Clip threads, remove pins, and press.

7. Place the postcard on the next line you will sew. In this example, it is the seamline between #1 and #3. Fold the paper back on the edge of the card. Because the previous stitching extends beyond the end, you will tear that stitching away from the foundation and that is OK. The fabric will remain sewn in the seam allowance, helping to reduce bulk. Place the Add-A-Quarter ruler on the fold and trim the fabric ¼" from this seamline.

Place postcard, fold paper, and trim.

8. Position the #3 fabric in the same way you positioned the #2 fabric piece and sew on the line between #1 and #3. Clip the threads and press open.

Position #3 fabric, sew, clip threads, and press.

9. The #4 and #5 pieces are half-square triangles. Trim the #4 seamline ¼" from the fold as before. Place the #4 triangle right side up on the blank side to approximate placement. Flip it over and place it right sides together with the just-trimmed seam, aligning the corner of the triangle with the triangle printed on the paper. Sew on the line, clip the threads, and press open.

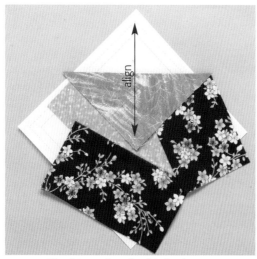

Trim #4 seamline, align #4 triangle, sew, clip threads, and press.

10. Complete the block by adding the final #5 triangle in the same way.

11. To trim the block, place the ¼" lines on the 6" x 6" square ruler on the solid sewing lines of 2 adjoining sides of the square. Trim the foundation and extending fabric exactly ¼" outside the sewing line and on the dashed line. Turn the block and trim the remaining 2 sides. Take care to do this accurately because an accurately trimmed block will join with other blocks and fabric squares more easily.

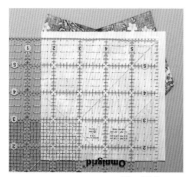

Trim ¼" from sewing lines.

Why Fold and Trim First?

The benefits of folding back on the next line you will sew in order to trim the previous fabric(s) ¼" from the line are worth stating.

1. The fold weakens the seamline, making paper removal even easier.

2. The fold line can be seen from the blank side of the foundation, making placement easier.

3. Because each fabric edge is trimmed parallel to the seamline, every piece placed on that edge will open exactly the same.

4. Positioning your fabrics ¼" from the edge will not waste fabric in the seam allowance, allowing the greatest portion of the fabric to fill the intended area.

5. The pretrimmed edge will help you place the next piece of fabric.

Paper-Piecing Tips

The following tips will assist you in sewing accurately and efficiently.

Fixing a Mistake

Mistakes do happen. The easiest way to remove a fabric piece is to place a piece of Scotch removable tape over the foundation seamline where you will remove the fabric piece. Pull the fabric piece back until the threads are exposed. Use the rotary point cutter to cut the threads as you keep tension on the fabric piece.

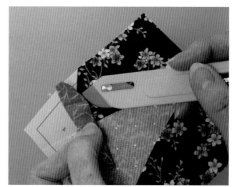

Place tape, pull fabric back, and cut threads.

After the piece is removed, lift up the fabric piece(s) from the foundation to allow the cut threads to move under the fabric pieces. Resew the fabric piece. The tape will become the new foundation and will perforate when it is time to remove the paper.

Assembly-Line Paper Piecing

When making multiple identical units, it is much faster to make them in an assembly-line fashion because you are repeating a step rather than thinking of the next step. Assembly-line piece up to twenty identical units by pinning all the #1 pieces, trimming the #1 pieces, and adding the #2 pieces one after the other without cutting the threads between units. Clip the threads, press the #2 pieces open, and trim the next seamlines. Continue assembly-line piecing until all identical units are completed.

Save Time Cutting Threads

A pair of curved pointed snips will cut the bobbin thread and the top thread at the same time. Pull the top thread up, and that will lift the bobbin thread so it can be snipped. When I do the math, I realize that this simple tip saves an enormous amount of time snipping threads. Just one 10-piece block has 20 bobbin threads. If you make 20 blocks, that would be 400 threads that will be cut with the top threads!

Snip top and bobbin threads at same time.

Save Steps Trimming Fabrics

When you are trimming subsequent fabric pieces that are not connected to each other, you can trim them both at the same time. In the following Unit 2 example, you can trim the seamlines for both #4 and #5 after you have paper-pieced through #3 because these numbers are not connected in any way. This permits you to trim them, sew them both, and press them both.

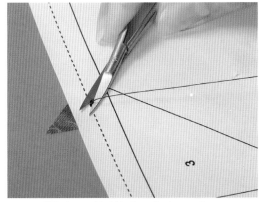

Unit 2

Pieced Units and Strip Piecing Option for Unit 29

Unit 29 contains a pieced unit signified by the "//" across the seamline between 3a and 3b. This is your cue to join the 3a fabric square and the 3b fabric square prior to piecing them to the foundation.

Unit 29
Join 3a and 3b fabrics prior to paper piecing them.

Position the seam of the pieced unit over the seamline, as seen looking through the blank side of the paper. Pin in place. Machine baste on the seamline about 1″ across the seam intersection and check for a good match prior to sewing the entire seam.

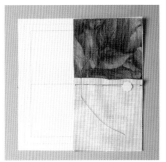

Check for a good match.

If you are making several units, you have the option to strip piece 2¾″-wide strips and crosscut them at 2¾″ intervals.

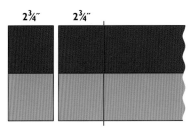

Crosscut at 2¾″ intervals.

Joining Foundations

Believe it or not, it is actually easier to join foundations accurately than it is to join two fabric squares, because the foundations don't stretch and the rigid quality of the paper will help align them.

1. Place 2 trimmed square foundations right sides together and tap the bottom edge to align them. Use your hands on the sides to align those edges. Pin at the beginning and the end of the seam away from the seam to be sewn. Pin the middle or any matching points along the seamline, again placing the pins away from the edge.

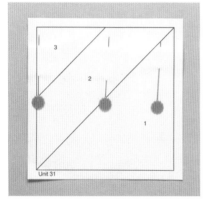

Pin squares.

If your foundations are triangle shapes, pin the right-angle corner first, then the 2 points, and finally any matching points.

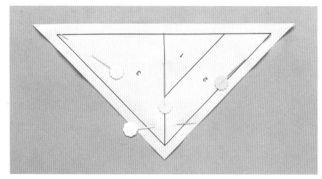

Pin squares.

2. To check that the seamlines are correctly aligned, place the seamline under the presser foot, drop the foot, and pierce the seamline with one hole. Raise the foot, remove the foundation, and check that the hole has gone through to the line on the foundation underneath. If the hole is above or below the line, adjust your pinning until the seamlines are aligned.

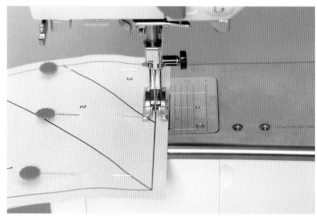

Pierce seamline to check alignment.

3. This next step is very important because it makes joining the blocks accurately a sure thing! Set the stitch length to a basting stitch, which is approximately a 3 (when the stitch ranges from 0 to 5) on your sewing machine. Machine baste the beginning, the middle or any match points, and the end without cutting the threads.

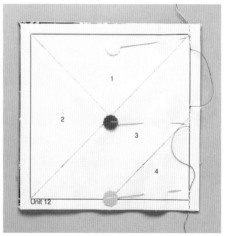

Machine baste.

4. Remove the pins and check that the block is basted accurately. If it is, reduce the stitch length back down to 1.5 and sew the seamline. If it is not, clip and remove the threads in the area that needs to be adjusted. Adjust, pin, baste, and check again.

Check for accuracy.

TIP When pinning units that have matching points and one or more seam intersections, pin the ends first, pin the matching points second, and pin the seam intersections last.

If you have joined two triangle-shape foundations, clip the points before pressing the foundation open.

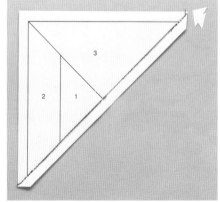

Clip triangle points.

Joining Foundations and Fabric

To join foundations to fabric squares, pin the fabric square to the foundation, right sides together. With the foundation side facing up, sew on the line. It is not necessary to machine baste first.

When assembling the paper units, fabric squares, and fabric borders, most of the time you will have a line on the foundation to sew on. However, occasionally there may be a short distance where there is no foundation and therefore no sewing line. In order to keep your ¼" seam allowance consistent, place four layers of masking tape ¼" to the right of the needle to create a sewing guide.

Pressing Seam Allowances

The general rule about pressing seam allowances is to press them in opposing directions. Always press from the fabric side of the block and do not put the iron on the paper side of the foundation because it will smear the ink on the foundation. When making the 9-patch star block using foundations for the four points, press the seam allowances toward the fabric squares.

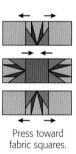

Press toward
fabric squares.

When joining the block horizontal rows, press the seam allowances toward the center of the block. This will permit you to rotate the blocks when joining them and have the middle seams go in opposing directions.

Press seams toward center.

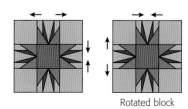

Rotated block

9-Patch Star Blocks

Each state star block is dedicated to the quilters in that state. When I selected the fabrics and the combination of units to produce each state star block, my goal was to provide variety rather than to tailor the star block design to a particular state theme. However, I must admit that I often related fabric choices to particular memories of a state.

The simple steps to make these star blocks are:

1. Make copies of the foundations indicated. Make 4 foundations for the star points, 4 foundations for the star corners, and 1 foundation for a star center. The unit foundations and cutting lists for the fabric pieces are on pages 82–101.

2. Assign color choices and create the cutting list (pages 16–17).

3. Cut the fabric pieces from your cutting list and label them with the number location and foundation unit. Don't forget to cut 4½" x 4½" fabric squares if fabric squares are used in the 4 corners or the center.

4. Paper piece and trim the foundation units (pages 20–23).

5. Assemble the units (and fabric squares if used) to complete the star block (pages 24–25).

Star 1, Alabama,
Unit 6

Star 2, Alaska,
Units 9, 28, and 39

Star 3, Arizona,
Units 16 and 36

Star 4, Arkansas,
Units 20, 21, and 34

Star 5, California,
Units 5, 22, and 33

Star 6, Colorado,
Units 14, 28, and 38

Star 7, Connecticut,
Units 7 and 31

Star 8, Delaware,
Units 1 and 24

Star 9, Florida,
Units 10 and 32

Star 10, Georgia,
Units 5 and 28

Star 11, Hawaii,
Units 12 and 33

Star 12, Idaho,
Units 15 and 30

Star 13, Illinois,
Units 11 and 39

Star 14, Indiana,
Units 8 and 27

Star 15, Iowa,
Units 10, 30, and 36

Star 16, Kansas,
Units 9 and 34

Star 17, Kentucky,
Units 11 and 35

Star 18, Louisiana,
Unit 20

Star 19, Maine,
Units 13 and 23

Star 20, Maryland,
Units 18 and 38

Star 21, Massachusetts,
Units 4 and 26

Star 22, Michigan,
Units 6 and 40

Star 23, Minnesota,
Units 3 and 29

Star 24, Mississippi,
Units 10, 24, and 40

Star 25, Missouri,
Units 5 and 39

Star 26, Montana,
Units 2 and 22

Star 27, Nebraska,
Units 6, 26, and 40

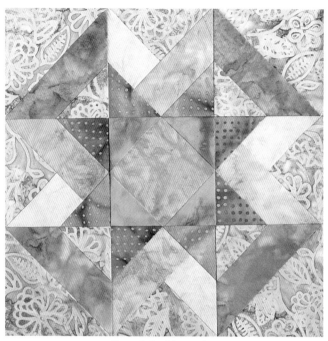

Star 28, Nevada,
Units 8, 21, and 31

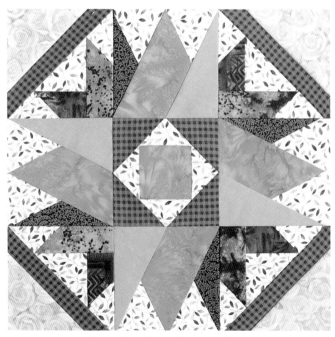

Star 29, New Hampshire,
Units 9, 24, and 35

Star 30, New Jersey,
Units 4, 25, and 36

Star 31, New Mexico,
Units 2, 24, and 34

Star 32, New York,
Units 16, 27, and 37

Star 33, North Carolina,
Units 8, 25, and 35

Star 34, North Dakota,
Units 13, 22, and 38

Star 35, Ohio,
Units 7, 26, and 33

Star 36, Oklahoma,
Units 4, 21, and 35

Star 37, Oregon,
Units 10 and 40

Star 38, Pennsylvania,
Units 5, 26, and 32

Star 39, Rhode Island,
Units 4, 29, and 40

Star 40, South Carolina,
Units 19, 27, and 34

Star 41, South Dakota,
Units 17 and 37

Star 42, Tennessee,
Units 7, 22, and 36

Star 43, Texas,
Units 2, 29, and 35

Star 44, Utah,
Units 14 and 25

Star 45, Vermont,
Units 8, 22, and 38

Star 46, Virginia,
Units 17, 23, and 31

Star 47, Washington,
Units 4, 30, and 34

Star 48, West Virginia,
Units 19 and 21

Star 49, Wisconsin,
Units 8 and 33

Star 50, Wyoming,
Units 6, 30, and 38

Quilt Projects

Bright Stars

Sensational Solids

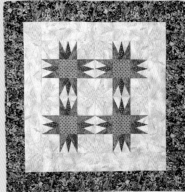

Stars of Spring

Star Roses

Flower Power

Autumn Stars

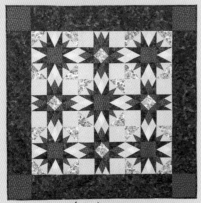

Blooming Stars

Floating Stars

Big and Little Stars

Triple Star Medallion

Star Crossed

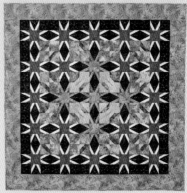

Tropical Punch

Bright Stars

Finished quilt size: 36″ x 36″
Finished block size: 12″ x 12″
Units: 10 and 35

Bright Stars, designed and pieced by Carol Doak, Windham, NH. Machine quilted by Kathryn Blais, 36″ x 36″, 2004.

Yardage Requirements

Yardage based on 42"-wide fabric

Floral print: 1⅛ yards for border and binding

Black: ⅓ yard for blocks

Blue: ¼ yard for blocks

Light blue: ¼ yard for blocks

Orange: ⅝ yard for blocks

Red: ⅓ yard for blocks

Green 1: ¼ yard for blocks

Green 2: ¼ yard for blocks

Gold: ¼ yard for blocks

Backing: 1⅛ yards

Batting: 40" x 40"

Cutting for Border and Binding

(Cut across the width of the fabric, selvage to selvage.)

FABRIC	No. to Cut	Size to Cut	Location
Floral print	2	6½" x 36½"	Top and bottom borders
	2	6½" x 24½"	Side borders
	4	2¼" x 40"	Binding

Cutting for Blocks

FABRIC	No. to Cut	Size to Cut	Location	Unit
Black	2	5½" x 5½" ⊠	1	10
	6	3½" x 3½" ⊠	4, 5	35
	6	3¼" x 3¼" ◻	1	35
Blue	6	4¼" x 4¼" ◻	7	35
Light blue	2	5½" x 5½" ⊠	1	10
	2	4¼" x 4¼" ◻	7	35
	2	3½" x 3½" ⊠	4, 5	35
	2	3¼" x 3¼" ◻	1	35
Orange	4	4½" x 4½"	Center squares	
	32	2½" x 5½"	4, 5	10
	4	1¾" x 3¾"	3	35
Red	16	2" x 5"	3	10
	4	1¾" x 2¾"	2	35
	16	1½" x 3½"	2	10
Green 1	12	1¾" x 3¾"	3	35
Green 2	12	1¾" x 2¾"	2	35
Gold	16	11/4" x 61/2"	6	35

Getting Started

1. Cut and label the fabric pieces for location, location numbers, and unit (pages 16–17).

2. Make 16 Unit 10 paper foundations (page 86) and 16 Unit 35 paper foundations (page 99).

Making the Units and Blocks

1. Make the units as shown.

Unit 10; Make 8

Unit 10; Make 8

Unit 35; Make 12

Unit 35; Make 4

2. Make the star blocks as shown.

Make 4

Make 4

Make 4

Make 4

Assembling the Quilt Top

1. Assemble the quilt top as shown.

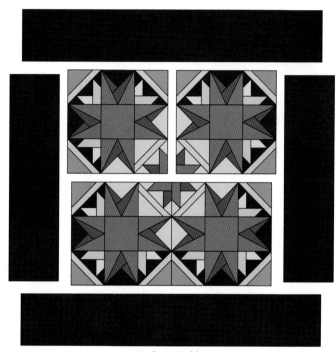
Quilt Assembly

2. Remove the paper. Layer, quilt, and bind the quilt. Refer to Quilt Finishing beginning on page 78.

Sensational Solids

Finished quilt size: 40" x 40"
Finished block size: 12" x 12"
Units: 16 and 24

Sensational Solids, designed and pieced by Carol Doak, Windham, NH. Machine quilted by Kathryn Blais, 40" x 40", 2004.

Yardage Requirements

Yardage based on 42"-wide fabric

Black solid: 1½ yards for blocks, outer border, and binding

Pink solid: ⅝ yard for inner border and border blocks

12 assorted solids: ⅛ yard each for blocks

Backing: 1¼ yards (If your fabric measures less than 44" wide, you will need 2½ yards.)

Batting: 44" x 44"

Cutting for Borders, Setting Pieces, and Binding

(Cut across the width of the fabric, selvage to selvage.)

Fabric	No. to Cut	Size to Cut	Location
Black	2	4½" x 40½"	Top and bottom outer borders
	2	4½" x 32½"	Side outer borders
	4	2¼" x 42"	Binding
*Pink	8	4½" x 8½"	Inner border
	4	4½" x 4½"	Inner border

*Cut the pieces for Unit 16 before cutting these inner border pieces.

Cutting for Blocks

Fabric	No. to Cut	Size to Cut	Location	Unit
Black	10	5½" x 5½" ⊠	4, 8	16
	16	4½" x 4½"	Block corner squares	
	4	3½" x 3½" ⊠	2, 3, 4, 5	24
Pink	2	5½" x 5½" ⊠	4	16
Asst. solids	24	3½" x 3½" ⊠	2, 3, 6, 7	16
	8	3¼" x 3¼" ◺	6, 7, 8, 9	24
	4	2¾" x 2¾"	1	24
	48	1¾" x 3¾"	1, 5	16

Getting Started

1. Cut and label the fabric pieces for location, location numbers, and unit (pages 16–17).

2. Make 24 Unit 16 paper foundations (page 89) and 4 Unit 24 paper foundations (page 93).

Making the Units and Blocks

1. Make the units as shown.

Unit 16; Make 16 for star blocks   Unit 16; Make 8 for inner border   Unit 24; Make 4 for star blocks

2. Make the star blocks as shown.

Make 8   Make 4

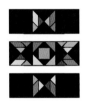

Make 4

Assembling the Quilt Top

1. Assemble the quilt top as shown.

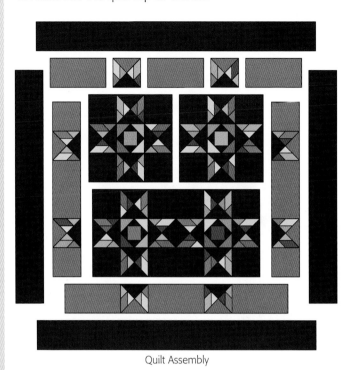

Quilt Assembly

2. Remove the paper. Layer, quilt, and bind the quilt. Refer to Quilt Finishing beginning on page 78.

Stars of Spring

Finished quilt size: 40″ x 40″
Finished block size: 12″ x 12″
Units: 1 and 38

Stars of Spring, designed and pieced by Carol Doak, Windham, NH. Machine quilted by Kathryn Blais, 40″ x 40″, 2004.

Yardage Requirements

Yardage based on 42"-wide fabric

Floral print: ⅞ yard for outer border and binding

Light green: 1¼ yards for inner border and blocks

Pink 1: ¼ yard for blocks

Pink 2: ½ yard for blocks

Green: ¼ yard for blocks

Yellow 1: ¼ yard for blocks

Yellow 2: ¼ yard for blocks

Backing: 1¼ yards (If your fabric measures less than 44" wide, you will need 2½ yards.)

Batting: 44" x 44"

Cutting for Borders and Binding

(Cut across the width of the fabric, selvage to selvage.)

Fabric	No. to Cut	Size to Cut	Location
Floral print	2	4½" x 40½"	Top and bottom outer borders
	2	4½" x 32½"	Side outer borders
	4	2¼" x 42"	Binding
Light green	4	4½" x 24½"	Inner border

Cutting for Blocks

Fabric	No. to Cut	Size to Cut	Location	Unit
Light green	4	4½" x 4½"	Block corner squares	
	16	2¾" x 2¾"	1	38
	32	2½" x 3½"	2, 3	1
	32	2¼" x 4½"	4, 5	38
Pink 1	4	4½" x 4½"	Block center squares	
Pink 2	32	2½" x 5½"	4, 5	1
Green	16	2" x 4¾"	1	1
Yellow 1	16	2¾" x 4¾"	3	38
Yellow 2	16	2" x 2¾"	2	38

Getting Started

1. Cut and label the fabric pieces for location, location numbers, and unit (pages 16–17).

2. Make 16 Unit 1 paper foundations (page 82) and 16 Unit 38 paper foundations (page 100).

Making the Units and Blocks

1. Make the units as shown.

Unit 1; Make 16   Unit 38; Make 16

2. Make the star blocks as shown.

Make 4   Make 4   Make 4

Make 4

Assembling the Quilt Top

1. Assemble the quilt top as shown.

Quilt Assembly

2. Remove the paper. Layer, quilt, and bind the quilt. Refer to Quilt Finishing beginning on page 78.

Star Roses

Finished quilt size: 48″ x 48″
Finished block size: 12″ x 12″
Units: 7, 18, and 33

Star Roses, designed and pieced by Carol Doak, Windham, NH. Machine quilted by Kathryn Blais, 48″ x 48″, 2004.

Yardage Requirements

Yardage based on 42"-wide fabric

Floral print: 1½ yards for border and binding

Black: 1⅛ yard for blocks

Red: ⅝ yard for blocks

Light red: ⅓ yard for blocks

Green: ¼ yard for blocks

Light green: ½ yard for blocks

Beige: ½ yard for blocks

Backing: 3 yards

Batting: 52" x 52"

Cutting for Border and Binding

(Cut down the length of the fabric parallel to selvages.)

Fabric	No. to Cut	Size to Cut	Location
Floral print	2	6½" x 48½"	Top and bottom borders
	2	6½" x 36½"	Side borders
	4	2¼" x 54"	Binding

Cutting for Blocks

Fabric	No. to Cut	Size to Cut	Location	Unit	Block
Black	4	5½" x 5½" ⊠	4	18	Star B
	18	5¼" x 5¼" ◸	4	33	Star A1, A2, B
	40	2½" x 4"	2, 3	7	Star A1, A2
Red	9	4½" x 4½"	Block center squares		Star A1, A2, B
	20	3¼" x 3¼" ◸	4, 5	7	Star A1, A2
	32	2" x 2"	1, 5	18	Star B
Light red	36	2¾" x 2¾"	1	33	Star A1, A2, B
Green	20	3¼" x 3¼" ◹	2, 3	33	Star A1, B
Light green	4	5½" x 5½" ⊠	8	18	Star B
	16	3¼" x 3¼" ◸	2, 3	33	Star A1, A2, B
Beige	16	3½" x 3½" ⊠	2, 3, 6, 7	18	Star B
	20	2¾" x 4¾"	1	7	Star A1, A2

Getting Started

1. Cut and label the fabric pieces for location, location numbers, unit, and block (pages 16–17).

2. Make 20 Unit 7 paper foundations (page 85), 16 Unit 18 paper foundations (page 90), and 36 Unit 33 paper foundations (page 98).

Making the Units and Blocks

1. Make the units as shown.

Unit 7; Make 20 for Stars A1 and A2 | Unit 18; Make 16 for Star B | Unit 33; Make 20 for Stars A1, A2, and B | Unit 33; Make 16 for Stars A1, A2, and B

2. Make Star A1 as shown.

Make 4   Make 4   Make 4

Star A1; Make 4

3. Make Star A2 as shown.

Make 2   Make 1

Star A2; Make 1

4. Make Star B as shown.

Make 4   Make 4   Make 4

Star B; Make 4

Assembling the Quilt Top

1. Assemble the quilt top as shown.

Quilt Assembly

2. Remove the paper. Layer, quilt, and bind the quilt. Refer to Quilt Finishing beginning on page 78.

Flower Power

Finished quilt size: 60″ x 60″
Finished block size: 12″ x 12″
Units: 5 and 39

Flower Power, designed and pieced by Carol Doak, Windham, NH. Machine quilted by Kathryn Blais, 60″ x 60″, 2004.

Yardage Requirements

Yardage based on 42"-wide fabric

Floral print: 1⅞ yards for outer border and binding

Black: 1 yard for inner border and sashing

Cream: 1¼ yards for blocks

Purple: ½ yard for blocks

Blue 1: ¼ yard for blocks

Blue 2: ¼ yard for blocks

Blue 3: ¼ yard for blocks

Blue 4: ¼ yard for blocks

Green: ⅝ yard for blocks

Green stripe: ⅝ yard for blocks

Backing: 3⅝ yards

Batting: 64" x 64"

Cutting for Borders, Sashing, and Binding

(Cut down the length of the fabric parallel to selvages.)

Fabric	No. to Cut	Size to Cut	Location
Floral print	2	6½" x 60½"	Top and bottom outer borders
	2	6½" x 48½"	Side outer borders
	4	2¼" x 65"	Binding

(Cut across the width of the fabric, selvage to selvage.)

Fabric	No. to Cut	Size to Cut	Location
Black	6	2½" x 12½"	Sashing
	2	2½" x 40½"	Sashing
	4	4½" x 40½"	Inner border

Cutting for Blocks

Fabric	No. to Cut	Size to Cut	Location	Unit
Cream	40	3¼" x 3¼" ◹	4, 5	39
	40	2¾" x 2¾"	1	39
	36	2¾" x 3½"	3	5
	36	2" x 2¾"	2	5
Purple	36	2¾" x 3¾"	1	5
Blues 1, 2, 3, 4	5 each	3¼" x 3¼" ◹	2	39
	10 each	2¾" x 4¾"	3	39
Green	9	4½" x 4½"	Center squares	
	72	1½" x 3½"	6, 7	5
Green stripe	72	1½" x 5½"	4, 5	5

Getting Started

1. Cut and label the fabric pieces for location, location numbers, and unit (pages 16–17).

2. Make 36 Unit 5 paper foundations (page 84) and 40 Unit 39 paper foundations (page 101).

Making the Units and Blocks

1. Make the units as shown.

Unit 39; Make 40 units using random placement of Blue 1, Blue 2, Blue 3, and Blue 4 for pieces 2 and 3

Unit 5; Make 36

2. Make the star blocks as shown.

Make 18

Make 9

Make 9

Assembling the Quilt Top

1. Assemble the quilt top as shown.

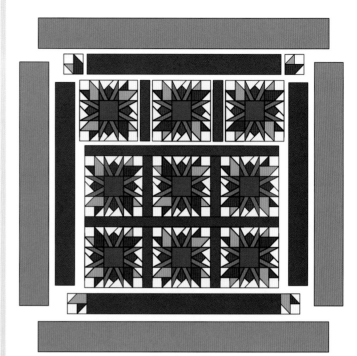

Quilt Assembly

2. Remove the paper. Layer, quilt, and bind the quilt. Refer to Quilt Finishing beginning on page 78.

Autumn Stars

Finished quilt size: 56" x 56"
Finished block size: 12" x 12"
Units: 17 and 32

Autumn Stars, designed and pieced by Carol Doak, Windham, NH. Machine quilted by Kathryn Blais, 56" x 56", 2004.

Yardage Requirements

Yardage based on 42"-wide fabric

Green: 1⅓ yards for border and binding

Floral print: ½ yard for center squares and corner squares

Orange solid: 1⅛ yards for setting pieces and blocks

Yellow: 1⅛ yards for blocks

Purple: ⅝ yard for blocks

Light green: ¾ yard for blocks

Backing: 3⅜ yards

Batting: 60" x 60"

Cutting for Border, Binding, and Corner Squares

(Cut down the length of the fabric, parallel to selvages.)

Fabric	No. to Cut	Size to Cut	Location
Green	4	6½" x 44½"	Border
	5	2¼" x 48"	Binding
Floral print	4	6½" x 6½"	Corner squares

Cutting for Setting Pieces

(Cut across the width of the fabric, selvage to selvage.)

Fabric	No. to Cut	Size to Cut	Location
Orange	12	4½" x 12½"	Setting pieces

Cutting for Blocks

Fabric	No. to Cut	Size to Cut	Location	Unit
Orange	10	4" x 4" ⊠	3	32
	20	2¾" x 2¾" ◻	2	32
Floral print	9	4½" x 4½"	Block center squares	
Yellow	38	5¼" x 5¼" ◻	5	17
			6	32
Purple	54	3¼" x 3¼" ◻	1, 3, 4	17
Light green	20	4" x 4" ⊠	4, 5	32
	18	3¼" x 3¼" ◻	2	17
	40	2¼" x 2¼"	1	32

Getting Started

1. Cut and label the fabric pieces for location, location numbers, and unit (pages 16–17).

2. Make 36 Unit 17 paper foundations (page 90) and 40 Unit 32 paper foundations (page 97).

Making the Units and Blocks

1. Make the units as shown.

Unit 17; Make 36 for
the star blocks

Unit 32; Make 36 for
the star blocks and 4 for
the corner squares

2. Make the star blocks as shown.

Make 18   Make 9

Make 9

Assembling the Quilt Top

1. Assemble the quilt top as shown.

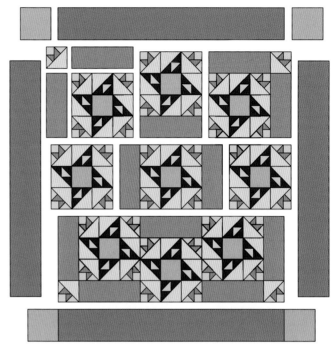

Quilt Assembly

2. Remove the paper. Layer, quilt, and bind the quilt. Refer to Quilt Finishing beginning on page 78.

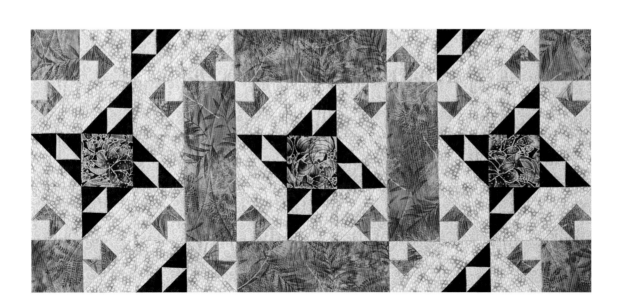

Blooming Stars

Finished quilt size: 48″ x 48″
Finished block size: 12″ x 12″
Units: 3, 21, and 34

Blooming Stars, designed and pieced by Carol Doak, Windham, NH. Machine quilted by Kathryn Blais, 48″ x 48″, 2004.

Yardage Requirements

Yardage based on 42"-wide fabric

Dark green: 2 yards for border, binding, and blocks

Dark pink: ⅞ yard for corner squares and blocks

Light green: 1¼ yards for blocks

Pink floral: ½ yard for blocks

Yellow: ⅜ yard for blocks

Backing: 3 yards

Batting: 52" x 52"

Cutting for Border, Binding, and Corner Squares

(Cut across the width of the fabric, selvage to selvage.)

FABRIC	NO. TO CUT	SIZE TO CUT	LOCATION
Dark green	4	6½" x 36½"	Border
	5	2¼" x 42"	Binding
Dark pink	4	6½" x 6½"	Corner squares

Cutting for Blocks

FABRIC	NO. TO CUT	SIZE TO CUT	LOCATION	UNIT	BLOCK
Dark green	72	2½" x 5½"	4, 5	3	Star A & B
Dark pink	5	4½" x 4½"	Center squares		Star B
	8	3¼" x 3¼" ◺	2, 3, 4, 5	21	Star A
	16	2¾" x 4¾"	1	3	Star A
	20	2" x 3½"	1	34	Star B
Light green	16	4½" x 4½"	Corner squares		Star A
	40	3¼" x 3¼"	2, 3	34	Star B
	72	2½" x 3"	2, 3	3	Star A & B
Pink floral	10	5¼" x 5¼" ◺	4	34	Star B
	4	3½" x 3½"	1	21	Star A
Yellow	20	2¾" x 4¾"	1	3	Star B

Getting Started

1. Cut and label the fabric pieces for location, location numbers, unit, and block (pages 16–17).

2. Make 36 Unit 3 paper foundations (page 83), 4 Unit 21 paper foundations (page 92), and 20 Unit 34 paper foundations (page 98).

Making the Units and Blocks

1. Make the units as shown.

Unit 3; Make 16 for Star A　　Unit 3; Make 20 for Star B　　Unit 21; Make 4 for Star A　　Unit 34; Make 20 for Star B

2. Make Star A as shown.

Make 8　　　　Make 4

Star A; Make 4

3. Make Star B as shown.

Make 10　　　　Make 5

Star B; Make 5

Assembling the Quilt Top

1. Assemble the quilt top as shown.

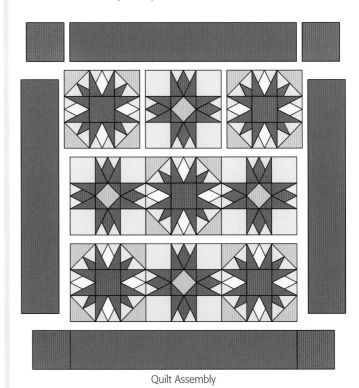

Quilt Assembly

2. Remove the paper. Layer, quilt, and bind the quilt. Refer to Quilt Finishing beginning on page 78.

Floating Stars

Finished quilt size: 72" x 72"
Finished block size: 12" x 12"
Unit: 11

Floating Stars, designed and pieced by Carol Doak, Windham, NH. Machine quilted by Kathryn Blais, 72" x 72", 2004.

Yardage Requirements

Yardage based on 42"-wide fabric

- **Floral print:** 2¼ yards for outer border and binding
- **Dark green:** 2⅛ yards for blocks
- **Pink:** 1⅜ yards for blocks
- **Light pink:** ⅝ yard for blocks
- **Light green:** 1¼ yards for blocks and setting squares
- **Purple print:** 1⅛ yards for blocks
- **Purple:** ½ yard for blocks
- **Backing:** 4¼ yards
- **Batting:** 76" x 76"

Cutting for Border and Binding

(Cut down the length of the fabric, parallel to selvages.)

FABRIC	NO. TO CUT	SIZE TO CUT	LOCATION
Floral print	2	6½" x 72½"	Top and bottom borders
	2	6½" x 60½"	Side borders
	4	2¼" x 75"	Binding

Cutting for Blocks and Setting Squares

FABRIC	NO. TO CUT	SIZE TO CUT	LOCATION
Dark green	64	4½" x 4½"	Block corner squares
	64	3" x 4"	3
	64	3" x 3"	2
Pink	16	4½" x 4½"	Block center squares
	128	2¼" x 4¾"	4, 5
Light pink	64	2¾" x 3½"	1
Light green	24	4½" x 4½"	Sashing setting squares
	48	3" x 4"	3
	48	3" x 3"	2
Purple print	9	4½" x 4½"	Sashing center squares
	96	2¼" x 4¾"	4, 5
Purple	48	2¾" x 3½"	1

Getting Started

1. Cut and label the fabric pieces for location, location numbers, and unit (pages 16–17).

2. Make 112 Unit 11 paper foundations (page 87).

Making the Units and Blocks

1. Make the units as shown.

Unit 11; Make 64 for
pink star blocks

Unit 11; Make 48 for
purple star blocks

2. Make the star blocks as shown.

Make 32   Make 16

Make 16

3. Make the vertical sashing strips as shown.

Make 12

4. Make the horizontal sashing strips as shown.

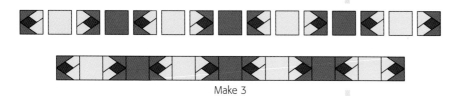

Make 3

Assembling the Quilt Top

1. Assemble the quilt top as shown.

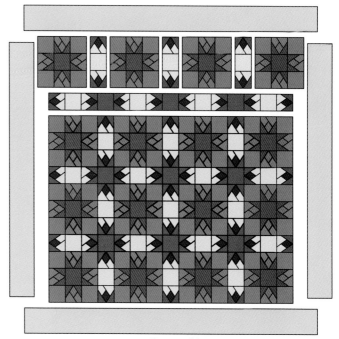

Quilt Assembly

2. Remove the paper. Layer, quilt, and bind the quilt. Refer to Quilt Finishing beginning on page 78.

Big and Little Stars

Finished quilt size: 68″ x 68″
Finished block size: 12″ x 12″
Units: 15 and 40

Big and Little Stars, designed and pieced by Carol Doak, Windham, NH. Machine quilted by Kathryn Blais, 68″ x 68″, 2004.

Yardage Requirements

Yardage based on 42"-wide fabric

Dark blue: 2¾ yards for blocks, outer border, and binding

White: 2¼ yards for setting squares, border units, and blocks

Blue floral: 1¼ yards for blocks

Light blue: ⅞ yard for blocks and border units

Light yellow: ½ yard for blocks and border units

Dark yellow: ⅓ yard for blocks and border units

Backing: 4 yards

Batting: 72" x 72"

Cutting for Border and Binding

(Cut down the length of the fabric, parallel to selvages.)

Fabric	No. to Cut	Size to Cut	Location
Dark blue	2	6½" x 68½"	Top and bottom borders
	2	6½" x 56½"	Side borders
	4	2¼" x 71"	Binding

Cutting for Blocks

Fabric	No. to Cut	Size to Cut	Location	Unit
Dark blue	64	1¼" x 6½"	4	15
	64	1¼" x 3½"	2	15
White	16	5½" x 5½" ⊠	1	15
	16	4½" x 4½"	Setting squares	
	100	4¼" x 4¼" ◻	4, 5	40
Blue floral	16	4¾" x 4¾" ⊠	3	15
	16	4½" x 4½"	Center squares	
	32	4½" x 4½" ◻	5	15
Light blue	100	2" x 5"	1	40
Light yellow	100	1¾" x 2¾"	3	40
Dark yellow	50	2¼" x 2¼" ◻	2	40

Getting Started

1. Cut and label the fabric pieces for location, location numbers, and unit (pages 16–17).

2. Make 64 Unit 15 paper foundations (page 89) and 100 Unit 40 paper foundations (page 101).

Making the Units and Blocks

1. Make the units as shown.

Unit 15; Make 64
for star blocks

Unit 40; Make 100
for star blocks and
inner border

2. Make the star blocks as shown.

Make 32   Make 16

Make 16

Assembling the Quilt Top

1. Assemble the quilt top as shown.

Quilt Assembly

2. Remove the paper. Layer, quilt, and bind the quilt. Refer to Quilt Finishing beginning on page 78.

Triple Star Medallion

Finished quilt size: 72″ x 72″
Finished block size: 12″ x 12″
Unit: 9

Triple Star Medallion, designed and pieced by Carol Doak, Windham, NH. Machine quilted by Kathryn Blais, 72″ x 72″, 2004.

Yardage Requirements

Yardage based on 42"-wide fabric

Black print: 2 yards for outer border and binding

Light red: 1½ yards for inner border and blocks

Dark red: 1¾ yards for blocks

Red 1: ½ yard for blocks

Red 2: ½ yard for blocks

Light green: 1⅜ yards for blocks

Green 1: ⅝ yard for blocks

Green 2: ⅝ yard for blocks

Green 3: ⅜ yard for blocks

Backing: 4¼ yards

Batting: 76" x 76"

Cutting for Borders and Binding

(Cut down the length of the fabric, parallel to selvages.)

FABRIC	NO. TO CUT	SIZE TO CUT	LOCATION
Black print	4	8½" x 48½"	Outer border
(Binding is cut across the width of the fabric.)	8	2¼" x 42"	Binding
Light red	4	4½" x 48½"	Inner border

Cutting for Blocks

FABRIC	NO. TO CUT	SIZE TO CUT	LOCATION	UNIT	BLOCK
Light red	8	4½" x 4½"	Center squares		Star A1
Dark red	48	4½" x 4½"	Corner squares		Star A2
	96	2½" x 3¼"	2, 4	9	Star A2
	32	1¾" x 4¾"	1	9	Star A1
Red 1	32	2½" x 5½"	5	9	Star A1
Red 2	32	2½" x 5½"	3	9	Star A1
Light green	32	4½" x 4½"	Corner squares		Star A1
	64	2½" x 3¼"	2, 4	9	Star A1
	48	1¾" x 4¾"	1	9	Star A2
Green 1	48	2½" x 5½"	5	9	Star A2
Green 2	48	2½" x 5½"	3	9	Star A2
Green 3	12	4½" x 4½"	Center squares		Star A2

Getting Started

1. Cut and label the fabric pieces for location, location numbers, and unit (pages 16–17).

2. Make 80 Unit 9 paper foundations (page 86).

Making the Units and Blocks

1. Make the units as shown.

Unit 9; Make 32 for Star A1   Unit 9; Make 48 for Star A2

2. Make Star A1 blocks as shown.

Make 16   Make 8

Star A1; Make 8

3. Make the Star A2 blocks as shown.

Make 24   Make 12

Star A2; Make 12

Assembling the Quilt Top

1. Assemble the quilt top as shown.

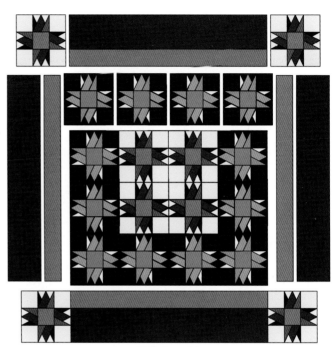

Quilt Assembly

2. Remove the paper. Layer, quilt, and bind the quilt. Refer to Quilt Finishing beginning on page 78.

Star Crossed

Finished quilt size: 60" x 60"
Finished block size: 12" x 12"
Units: 7 and 40

Star Crossed, designed and pieced by Carol Doak, Windham, NH. Machine quilted by Kathryn Blais, 60" x 60", 2004.

Yardage Requirements

Yardage based on 42"-wide fabric

Black floral: 1¾ yards for outer border and binding

Black: 1½ yards for blocks

White: ⅔ yard for blocks

Light green: ⅝ yard for blocks

Dark green: ⅔ yard for blocks

Light pink: ½ yard for blocks

Dark pink: ⅝ yard for blocks

Purple: ⅝ yard for blocks

Backing: 3⅝ yards

Batting: 64" x 64"

Cutting for Border and Binding

(Cut down the length of the fabric, parallel to selvages.)

Fabric	No. to Cut	Size to Cut	Location
Black floral	2	6½" x 60½"	Top and bottom borders
	2	6½" x 48½"	Side borders
	4	2¼" x 63"	Binding

Cutting for Blocks and Setting Squares

Fabric	No. to Cut	Size to Cut	Location	Unit	Block
Black	48	4¼" x 4¼" ◩	4, 5	40	1, 2, 3, 4
	96	2½" x 4"	2, 3	7	1, 2, 3, 4
White	16	4¼" x 4¼" ◩	4, 5	40	2, 4
	32	2½" x 4"	2, 3	7	2, 4
Light green	64	2" x 5"	1	40	1, 2, 3, 4
Dark green	64	3¼" x 3¼" ◩	4, 5	7	1, 2, 3, 4
Light pink	32	2¼" x 2¼" ◩	2	40	1, 2, 3, 4
	64	1¾" x 2¾"	3	40	1, 2, 3, 4
Dark pink	8	4½" x 4½"	Center squares		1, 2
	32	2¾" x 4¾"	1	7	1, 2
Purple	8	4½" x 4½"	Center squares		3, 4
	32	2¾" x 4¾"	1	7	3, 4

Getting Started

1. Cut and label the fabric pieces for location, location numbers, and unit (pages 16–17).

2. Make 64 Unit 7 paper foundations (page 85) and 64 Unit 40 paper foundations (page 101).

Making the Units and Blocks

1. Make the units as shown.

Unit 7; Make 24 for Stars 1 and 2

Unit 7; Make 8 for Star 2

Unit 7; Make 24 for Stars 3 and 4

Unit 7; Make 8 for Star 4

2. Make the units as shown.

Unit 40; Make 40 for Stars1, 2, 3, and 4

Unit 40; Make 8 for Stars 2 and 4

Unit 40; Make 8 for Stars 2 and 4

Unit 40; Make 8 for Stars 2 and 4

3. Make Star 1 blocks as shown.

Make 8   Make 4

Star 1; Make 4

4. Make Star 2 as shown.

Make 4   Make 4   Make 4

Star 2; Make 4

5. Make Star 3 as shown.

Make 8   Make 4

Star 3; Make 4

6. Make Star 4 as shown.

Make 4   Make 4   Make 4

Star 4; Make 4

Assembling the Quilt Top

1. Assemble the quilt top as shown.

Quilt Assembly

2. Remove the paper. Layer, quilt, and bind the quilt. Refer to Quilt Finishing beginning on page 78.

Tropical Punch

Finished quilt size: 72″ x 72″
Finished block size: 12″ x 12″
Units: 2 and 31

Tropical Punch, designed and pieced by Carol Doak, Windham, NH. Machine quilted by Kathryn Blais, 72″ x 72″, 2004.

Yardage Requirements

Yardage based on 42"-wide fabric

- **Green:** 2¾ yards for blocks, border, and binding
- **Black:** 2½ yards for blocks
- **Medium pink:** ⅜ yard for blocks
- **Light pink:** 1⅛ yards for blocks
- **Fuchsia:** 1⅓ yards for blocks
- **Blue:** ½ yard for blocks
- **Yellow:** ⅓ yard for blocks
- **Multicolor print:** ⅞ yard for blocks
- **Backing:** 4¼ yards
- **Batting:** 76" x 76"

Cutting for Border and Binding

Fabric	No. to Cut	Size to Cut	Location
Green	2	6½" x 72½"	Top and bottom borders
	2	6½" x 60½"	Side borders
	4	2¼" x 76"	Binding

Cutting for Blocks

Fabric	No. to Cut	Size to Cut	Location	Unit	Block
Green	5	4½" x 4½"	Center squares		1, 2
	40	1½" x 5½"	2, 3	2	1, 2
Black	100	4¾" x 4¾"	1	2	1, 2, 3, 4, 5, 6
	36	4½" x 4½"	Corner squares		4, 5, 6
Medium pink	2	5¼" x 5¼" ◨	1	31	1
	8	4½" x 4½"	Corner squares		2
Light pink	160	1½" x 5½"	2, 3	2	3, 4, 5, 6
Fuchsia	20	4½" x 4½"	Center squares		3, 4, 5, 6
	200	1½" x 3½"	4, 5	2	1, 2, 3, 4, 5, 6
Blue	32	2" x 6½"	2	31	1, 3, 4, 5
Yellow	16	3¼" x 3¼" ◨	3	31	1, 3, 4, 5
Multicolor	14	5¼" x 5¼" ◨	1	31	3, 4, 5
	24	4½" x 4½"	Corner squares		2, 6

Getting Started

1. Cut and label the fabric pieces for location, location numbers, and unit (pages 16–17).

2. Make 100 Unit 2 paper foundations (page 82) and 32 Unit 31 paper foundations (page 97).

Making the Units and Blocks

1. Make the units as shown.

Unit 2; Make 20 for
Stars 1 and 2

Unit 2; Make 80 for
Stars 3, 4, 5, and 6

2. Make the units as shown.

Unit 31; Make 28 for
Stars 3, 4, and 5

Unit 31; Make 4
for Star 1

3. Make Star 1 as shown.

Make 2   Make 1

Star 1; Make 1

4. Make Star 2 as shown.

Make 4   Make 4   Make 4

Star 2; Make 4

5. Make Star 3 as shown.

Make 8   Make 4

Star 3; Make 4

6. Make Star 4 as shown.

Make 4   Make 4   Make 4

Star 4; Make 4

7. Make Star 5 as shown.

Make 4   Make 4   Make 4

Star 5; Make 4

8. Make Star 6 as shown.

Make 8   Make 8   Make 8

Star 6; Make 8

Assembling the Quilt Top

1. Assemble the quilt top as shown.

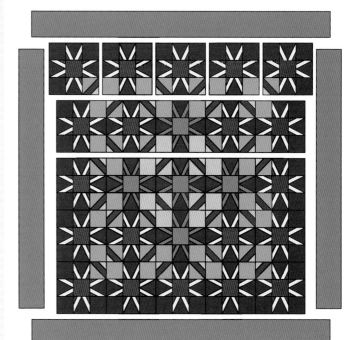

Quilt Assembly

2. Remove the paper. Layer, quilt, and bind the quilt. Refer to Quilt Finishing beginning on page 78.

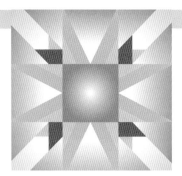

Quilt Finishing

Quilt Assembly

Do not remove the paper until your project is complete. It will stabilize any off-grain edges and will give you a sewing line.

To assemble the star blocks and borders to create the quilt projects, follow the layout illustrations at the end of each set of quilt directions. Press seam allowances in opposing directions and toward the borders.

Removing Paper

Once the quilt top is complete, remove the paper. Start at the outside edge of your project and tug against the lines of stitching. The paper should pull away easily. I find it easiest to remove the largest pieces first and then go back to remove the strips along the seam allowances with a pair of tweezers.

Once the majority of the paper is removed, take the quilt outside and give it a good shake. This will remove pieces still clinging on. Don't be concerned with removing every tiny bit of paper. Those bits will just add to the warmth of the quilt.

Removing the paper is one of those activities I reserve for times when I can keep my hands busy while doing something else—like listening to music, watching TV, riding in the car, or chatting on the phone. I have even been known to enlist the help of my perfect granddaughter to remove paper. At first she wasn't enjoying the process, but after I showed her how to tug against the stitching lines, she had a ball!

Layer, Baste, and Quilt

Once the paper is removed, the quilt top, batting, and backing are layered. The backing and batting should be 2″ larger than the quilt top all the way around. If the quilt width requires more than one width of fabric, seam two lengthwise cuts. Press the seam allowances open.

My perfect granddaughter helping me remove paper.

Place the backing wrong side up. Place the batting on top of the backing. Position the quilt top on top, right side up.

Hand baste or pin baste the three layers together. Begin in the center and baste in a grid with lines approximately 4″ apart, working from the center toward the outside edge.

Your quilt is now ready for hand or machine quilting. The quilting designs used in the quilt photos offer inspiration—or use your own creative ideas to enhance your quilts.

Sleeve

If you plan to hang your quilt, now is the time to attach the sleeve. The sleeve will provide a place for a rod to hang the quilt.

1. Cut a piece of fabric (or join fabric pieces) to create a strip that is 1″ shorter than the width of the quilt and 12″ wide.

2. Fold under ¼″ on each short edge, and then fold a second time. Press and stitch to hem the edges.

3. Fold the sleeve in half along the long sides, with wrong sides together, and press.

4. Position the cut edges of the sleeve centered on the top edge of the quilt, then pin and machine baste in place ⅛″ from the edge. This edge will be secured when the binding is attached.

5. Hand appliqué the long folded edge to the backing of the quilt with matching thread.

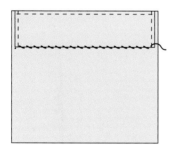

Center the sleeve along the top edge of quilt. Baste at the top edge and hand appliqué the bottom folded edge.

Binding

1. Join the ends of the 2¼″-wide strips using a 45° seam, trim ¼″ from the seam, and clip off the "dog-ears." Press the seam allowance open.

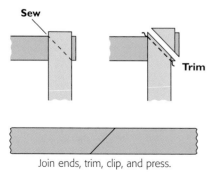

Join ends, trim, clip, and press.

2. At the beginning of the strip, mark three 45° lines ¼″ apart as shown, on the **wrong** side of the fabric, using a ruler and pencil. Cut on the line closest to the end.

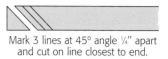

Mark 3 lines at 45° angle ¼″ apart and cut on line closest to end.

3. Fold the binding strip in half wrong sides together and press.

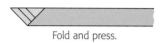

Fold and press.

4. Place the beginning of the strip on the top of the outside edge of the quilt, matching the raw edges, and pin in place. Begin sewing approximately 6″ from the beginning of the strip and ¼″ from the edge, using a walking foot or even feed foot. Stop sewing and backstitch ¼″ from the corner. Clip the threads.

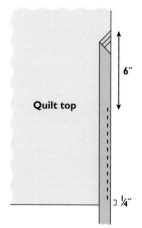

Quilt top

6″

¼″

Place strip, pin, and stitch.

5. Fold the binding up at a 90° angle, making the raw edge parallel with the raw edge of the quilt.

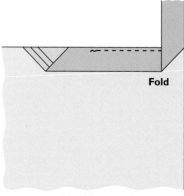

Fold

Fold binding at 90°.

6. Then fold down, making the fold flush with the top edge of the corner. Begin stitching the second side using a ¼" seam.

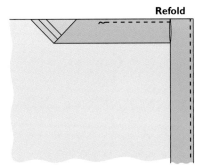

Fold down and stitch.

7. To seam the ends, stop stitching about 6" from the beginning of the binding strip. Open the end of the binding and place it under the beginning of the binding strip. Make a pencil mark on the wrong side of the end strip at the second line of the beginning of the binding. Move the end binding strip and mark a 45° line at the pencil marking. Mark a second line ¼" away toward the sewn portion of the binding strip.

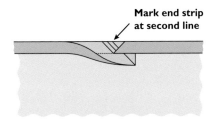

Position binding ends and mark lines.

8. Move the end of the binding strip away from the quilt top and trim on the line closest to the end of the strip. Place the ends of the binding strip right sides together and pin, matching the lines that are ¼" from the cut ends. Sew on the line and press the seam allowance open.

Cut on line, pin, and stitch.

9. Fold and press the joined strip wrong sides together. Place the edge of the strip back on the quilt top and sew to the beginning.

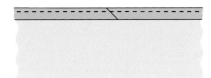

Fold, press, and stitch.

10. Fold the binding strip to the back of the quilt and blind-stitch in place. Miter the corners as shown.

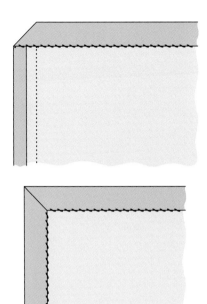

Fold, press, and stitch.

Labeling Your Quilt

Don't leave future generations wondering who made your lovely quilt or why, when, and where it was made. Take the time to make a simple label for your quilt, including whatever information you would like. I often use my printer to print this information on fabric and then foundation piece around this fabric to create my labels. You can use one of the center unit foundations to create your label. In the following example, Unit 26 was used as a label.

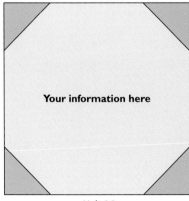

Your information here

Unit 26

Don't leave future generations wondering who made your lovely quilt or why, when, and where it was made.

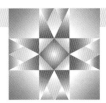

Foundation Units and Cutting Lists

Point Units

Unit 1

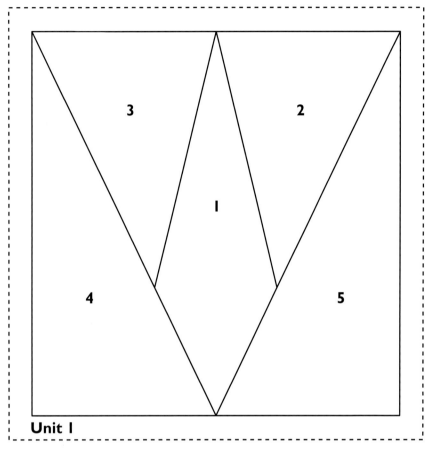

Unit I

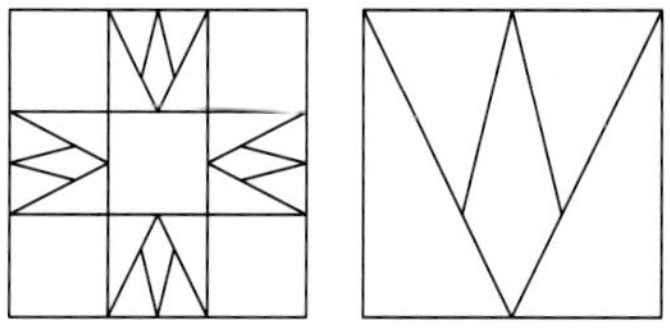

Cutting List for Unit 1

Location	Size to Cut	4 Units
1	2″ x 4¾″	4
2, 3	2½″ x 3½″	8
4, 5	2½″ x 5½″	8

Unit 2

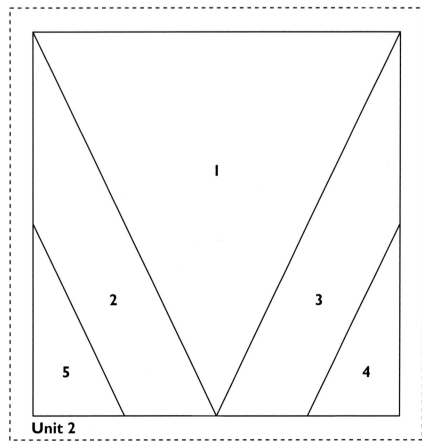

Unit 2

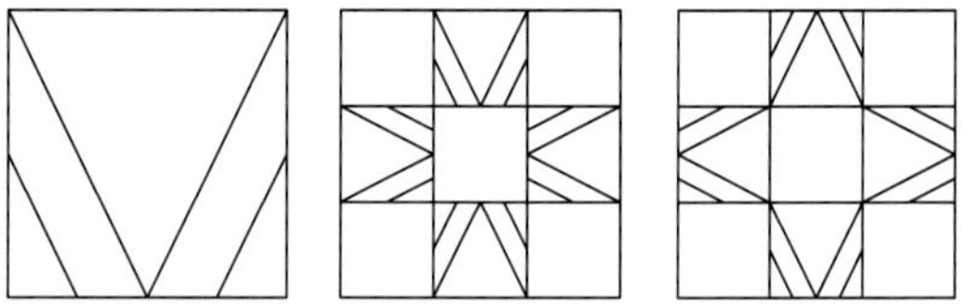

Cutting List for Unit 2

Location	Size to Cut	4 Units
1	4¾″ x 4¾″	4
2, 3	1½″ x 5½″	8
4, 5	1½″ x 3½″	8

Unit 3

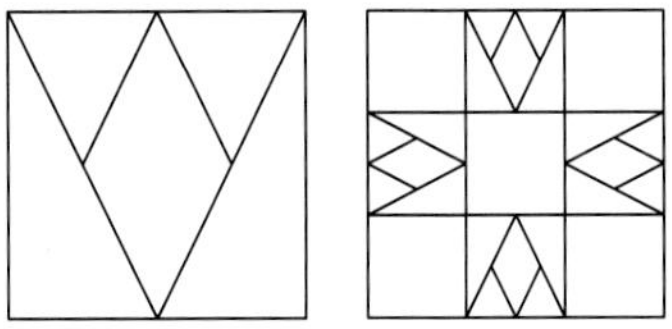

Cutting List for Unit 3

Location	Size to Cut	4 Units
1	2¾″ x 4¾″	4
2, 3	2½″ x 3″	8
4, 5	2½″ x 5½″	8

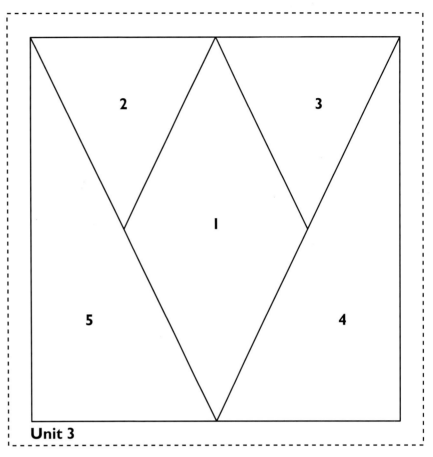

Unit 3

Unit 4

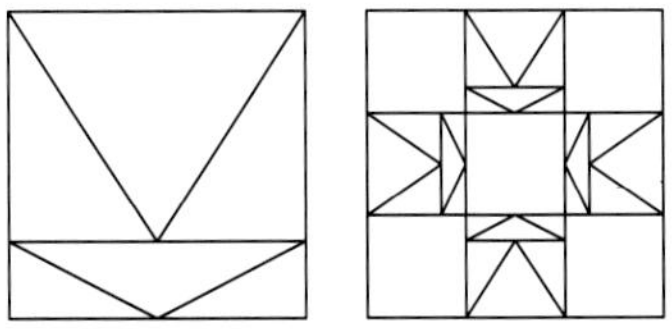

Cutting List for Unit 4

Location	Size to Cut	4 Units
1	3¾″ x 4¾″	4
2, 3	2¼″ x 4½″	8
4	1¾″ x 4¾″	4
5, 6	1½″ x 3¼″	8

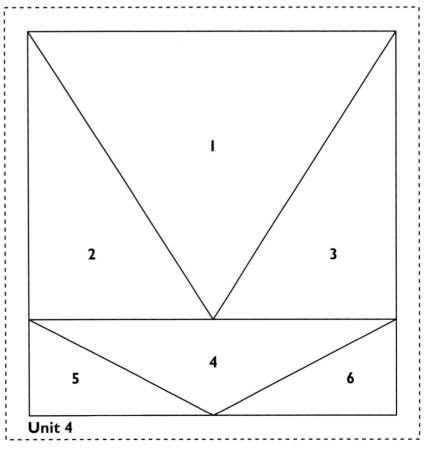

Unit 4

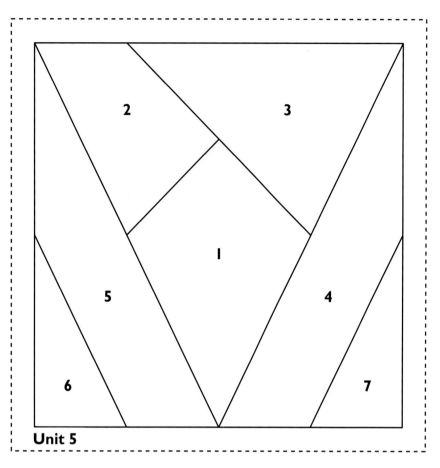

Unit 5

Unit 5

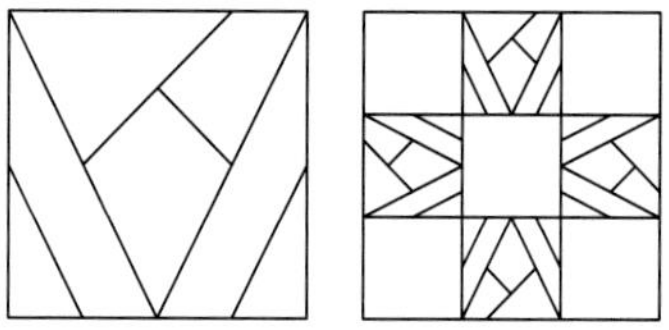

Cutting List for Unit 5

Location	Size to Cut	4 Units
1	2¾" x 3¾"	4
2	2" x 2¾"	4
3	2¾" x 3½"	4
4, 5	1½" x 5½"	8
6, 7	1½" x 3½"	8

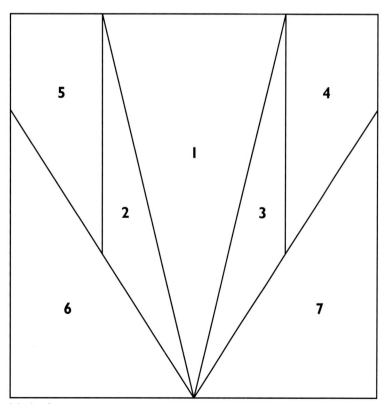

Unit 6

Unit 6

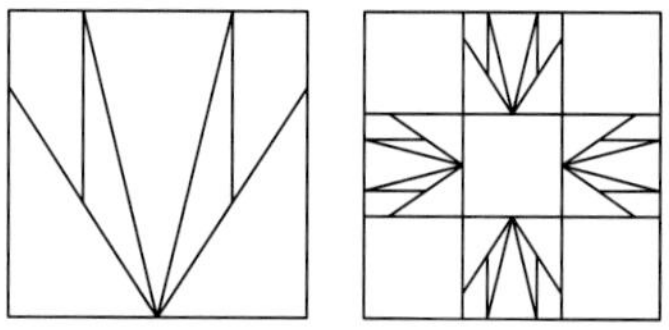

Cutting List for Unit 6

Location	Size to Cut	4 Units
1	2¾" x 4¾"	4
2, 3	1¼" x 5"	8
4, 5	1¾" x 3¼"	8
6, 7	2¼" x 4¾"	8

Unit 7

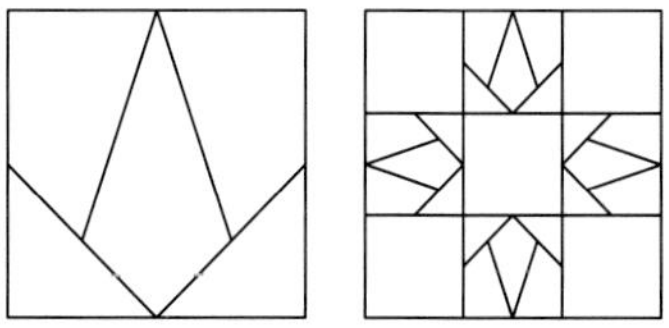

Cutting List for Unit 7

Location	Size to Cut	4 Units
1	2¾" x 4¾"	4
2, 3	2½" x 4"	8
4, 5	3¼" x 3¼" ◻	4

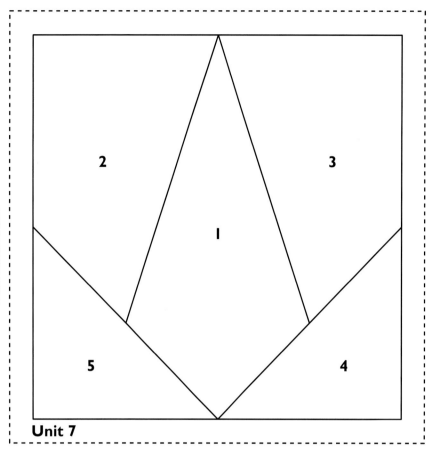

Unit 7

Unit 8

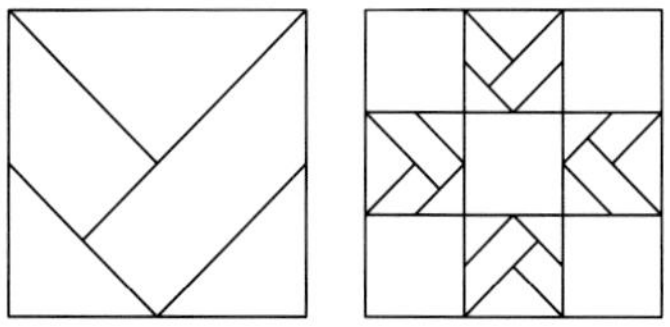

Cutting List for Unit 8

Location	Size to Cut	4 Units
1	5½" x 5½" ⊠	1
2	2" x 3½"	4
3	2" x 5"	4
4, 5	3¼" x 3¼" ◻	4

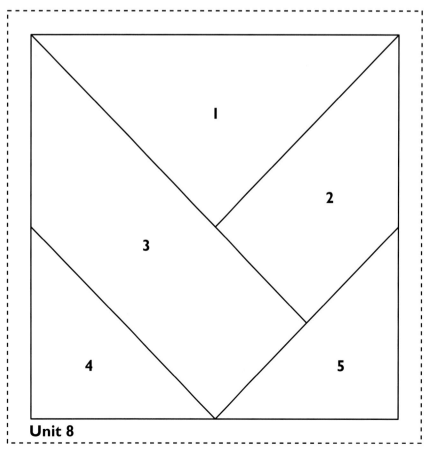

Unit 8

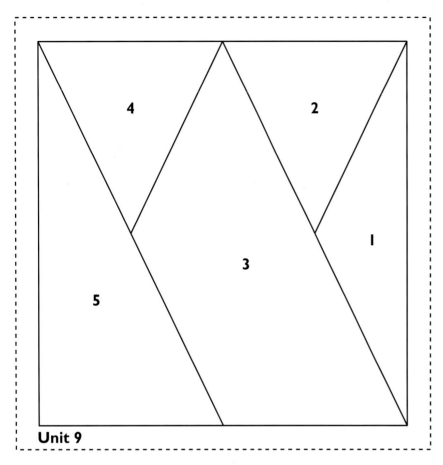

Unit 9

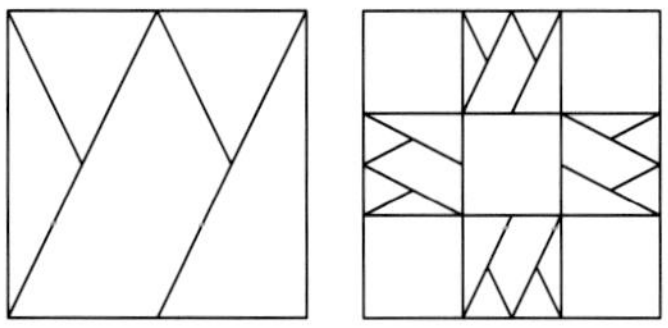

Unit 9

Cutting List for Unit 9

Location	Size to Cut	4 Units
1	1¾" x 4¾"	4
2, 4	2½" x 3¼"	8
3, 5	2½" x 5½"	8

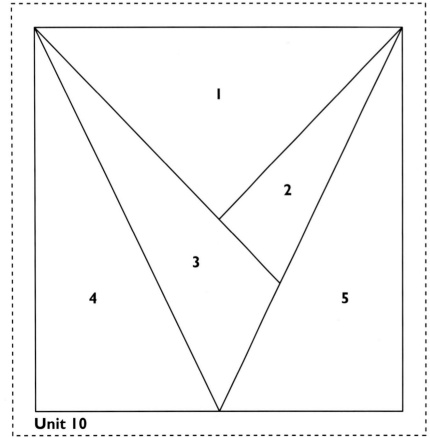

Unit 10

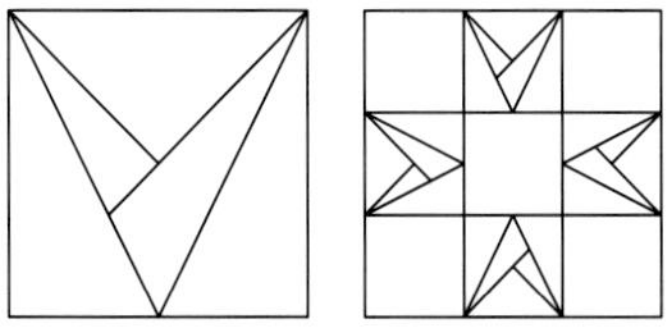

Unit 10

Cutting List for Unit 10

Location	Size to Cut	4 Units
1	5½" x 5½" ⊠	1
2	1½" x 3½"	4
3	2" x 5"	4
4, 5	2½" x 5½"	8

Unit 11

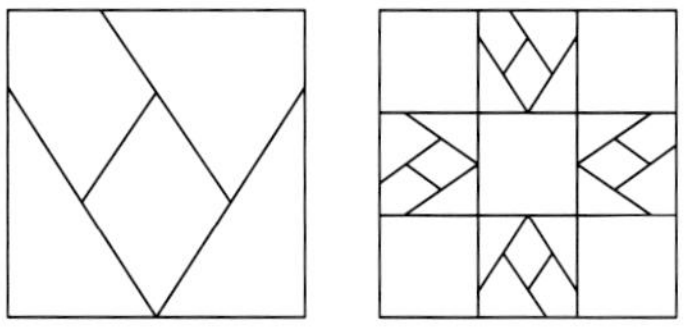

Cutting List for Unit 11

Location	Size to Cut	4 Units
1	2¾″ x 3½″	4
2	3″ x 3″	4
3	3″ x 4″	4
4, 5	2¼″ x 4¾″	8

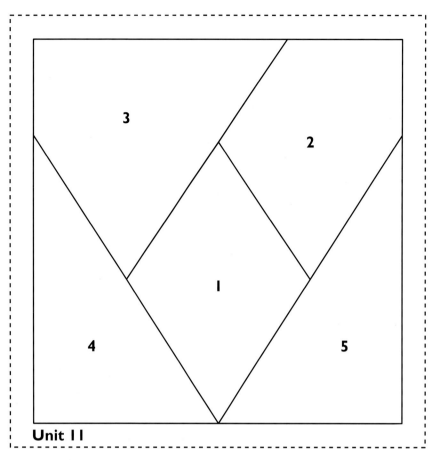

Unit 11

Unit 12

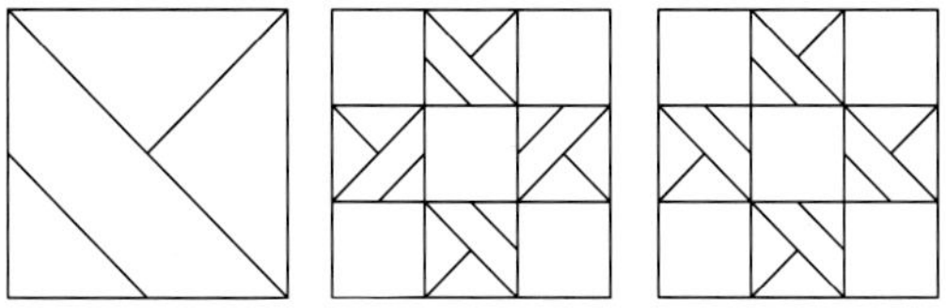

Cutting List for Unit 12

Location	Size to Cut	4 Units
1, 2	5½″ x 5½″ ⊠	2
3	2″ x 6½″	4
4	3¼″ x 3¼″ ◻	2

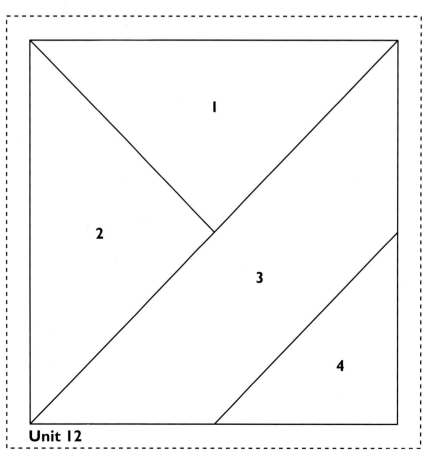

Unit 12

Unit 13

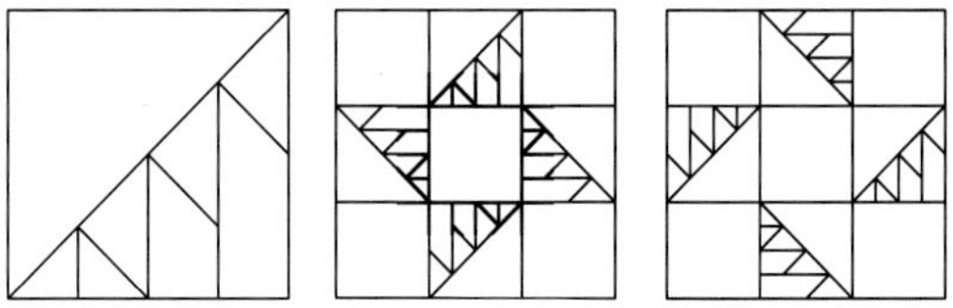

Cutting List for Unit 13

Location	Size to Cut	4 Units
1, 2	2¼″ x 2¼″ ◺	4
3, 5, 7	3½″ x 3½″ ⊠	3
4	1¾″ x 2¾″	4
6	1¾″ x 3¾″	4
8	5¼″ x 5¼″ ◺	2

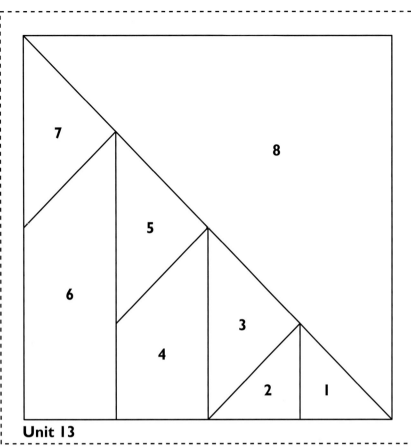

Unit 14

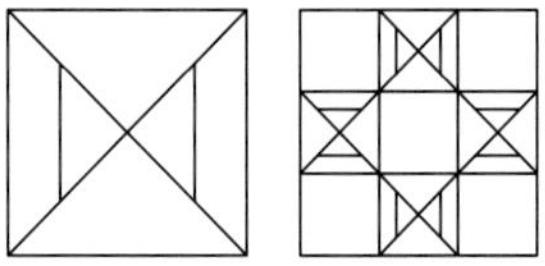

Cutting List for Unit 14

Location	Size to Cut	4 Units
1, 4	3¾″ x 3¾″ ⊠	2
2, 5	1½″ x 4¾″	8
3, 6	5½″ x 5½″ ⊠	2

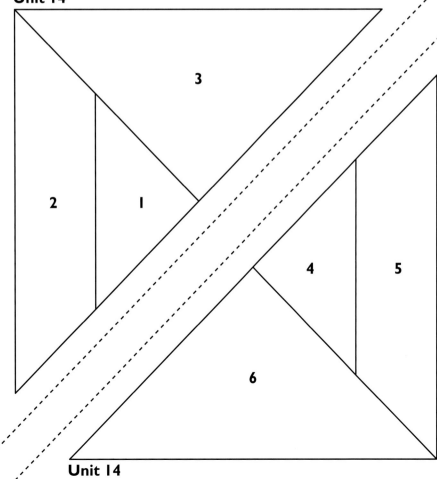

Unit 15

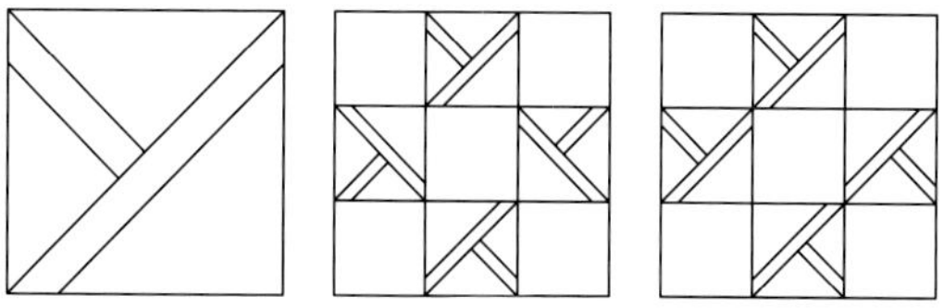

Cutting List for Unit 15

Location	Size to Cut	4 Units
1	5½" x 5½" ⊠	1
2	1¼" x 3½"	4
3	4¾" x 4¾" ⊠	1
4	1¼" x 6½"	4
5	4½" x 4½" ◺	2

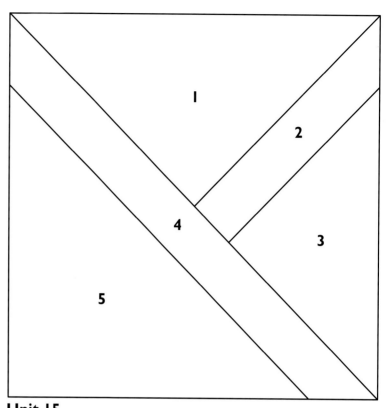

Unit 15

Unit 16

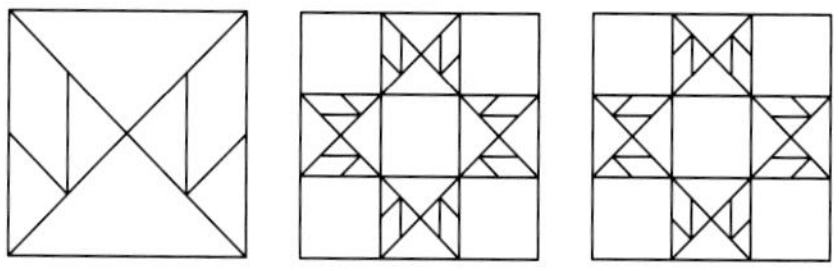

Cutting List for Unit 16

Location	Size to Cut	4 Units
1, 5	1¾" x 3¾"	8
2, 3, 6, 7	3½" x 3½" ⊠	4
4, 8	5½" x 5½" ⊠	2

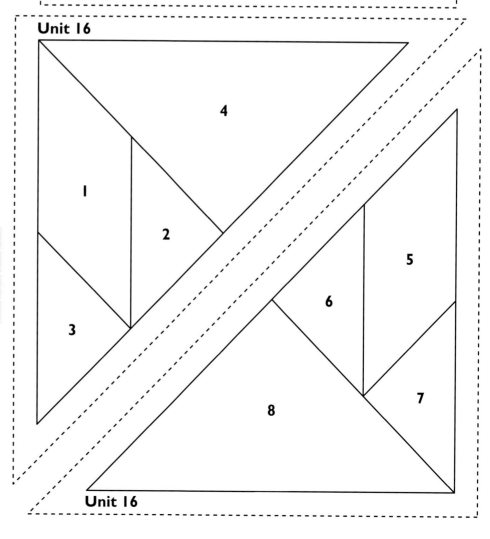

Unit 16

Unit 16

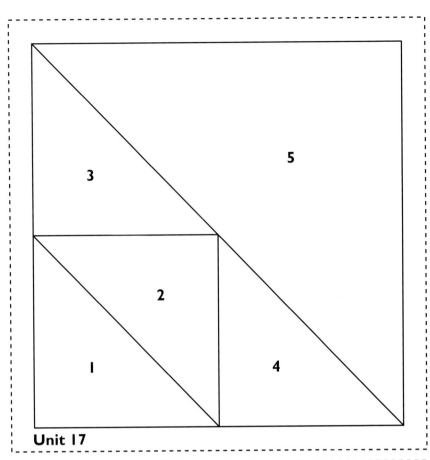

Unit 17

Unit 17

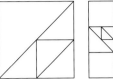

Cutting List for Unit 17

Location	Size to Cut	4 Units
1, 2, 3, 4	3¼" x 3¼" ◩	8
5	5¼" x 5¼" ◩	2

Unit 18

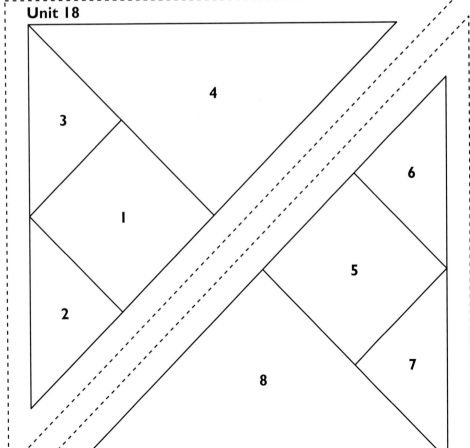

Unit 18

Cutting List for Unit 18

Location	Size to Cut	4 Units
1, 5	2" x 2"	8
2, 3, 6, 7	3½" x 3½" ⊠	4
4, 8	5½" x 5½" ⊠	2

Unit 18

Unit 19

Cutting List for Unit 19

Location	Size to Cut	4 Units
1, 2	2¼" x 2¼" ◺	4
3, 4, 5, 6, 7	3½" x 3½" ⊠	5
8	5¼" x 5¼" ◺	2
9	3¼" x 3¼" ◺	2

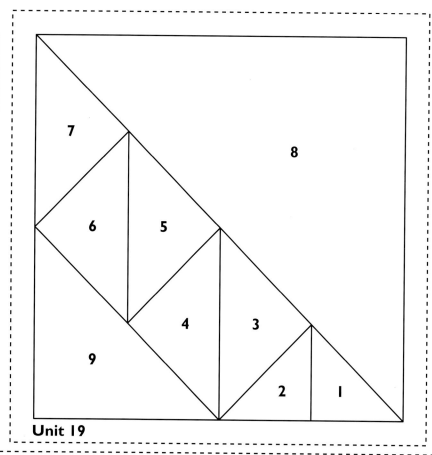

Unit 19

Unit 20

Cutting List for Unit 20

Location	Size to Cut	4 Units
1–5, 10–14	2¼" x 2¼" ◺	20
6, 7, 15, 16	2½" x 2½" ⊠	4
8, 17	3½" x 3½" ⊠	2
9, 18	5½" x 5½" ⊠	2

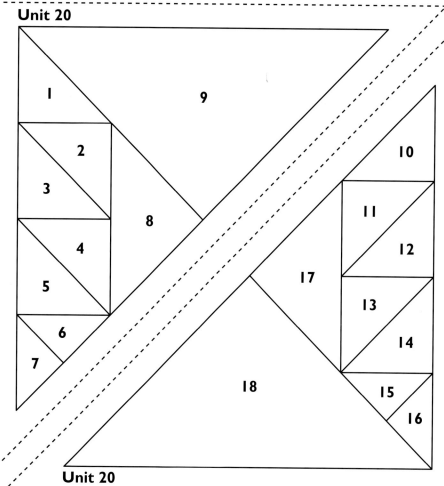

Unit 20

Unit 20

Center Units

Unit 21

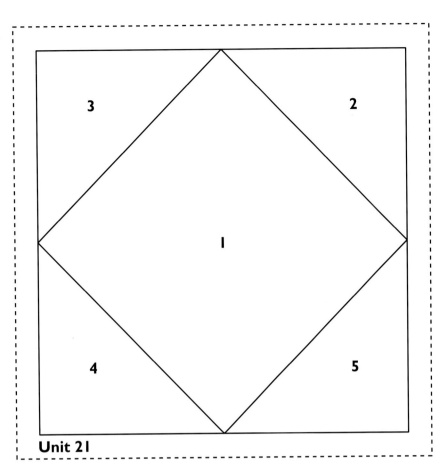

Unit 21

Cutting List for Unit 21

Location	Size to Cut	1 Unit
1	3½" x 3½"	1
2, 3, 4, 5	3¼" x 3¼" ◹	2

Unit 22

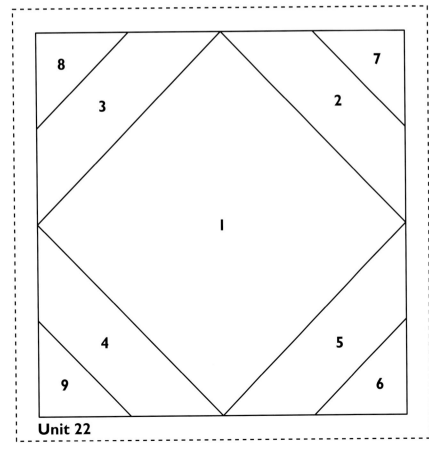

Unit 22

Cutting List for Unit 22

Location	Size to Cut	1 Unit
1	3½" x 3½"	1
2, 3, 4, 5	1½" x 3½"	4
6, 7, 8, 9	2¼" x 2¼" ◹	2

Unit 23

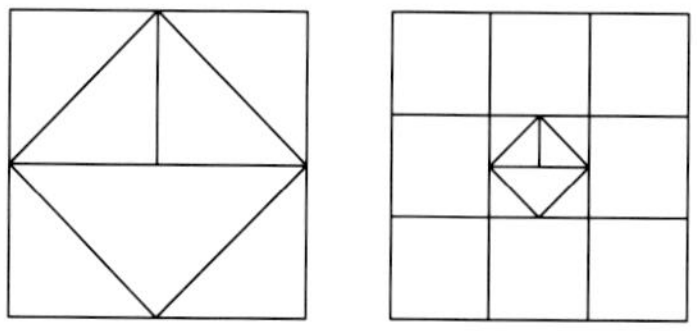

Cutting List for Unit 23

Location	Size to Cut	1 Unit
1, 2, 4–7	3¼" x 3¼" ◺	3
3*	2¾" x 4¾"	1

*If making multiple blocks, cut a square 5½" x 5½" ⊠ to produce 4 triangles.

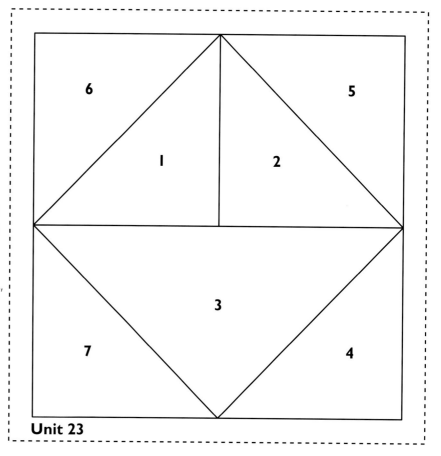

Unit 23

Unit 24

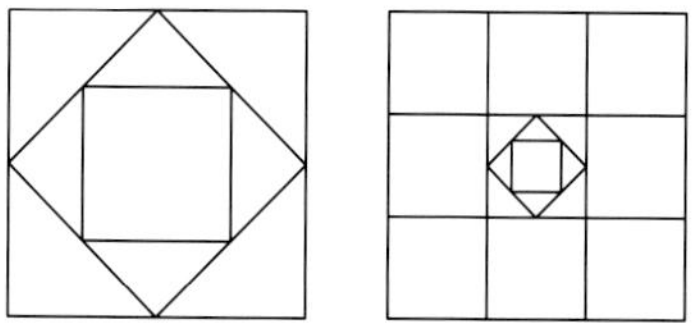

Cutting List for Unit 24

Location	Size to Cut	1 Unit
1	2¾" x 2¾"	1
2, 3, 4, 5	3½" x 3½" ⊠	1
6, 7, 8, 9	3¼" x 3¼" ◺	2

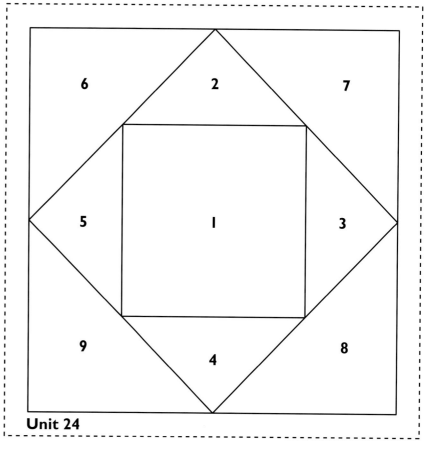

Unit 24

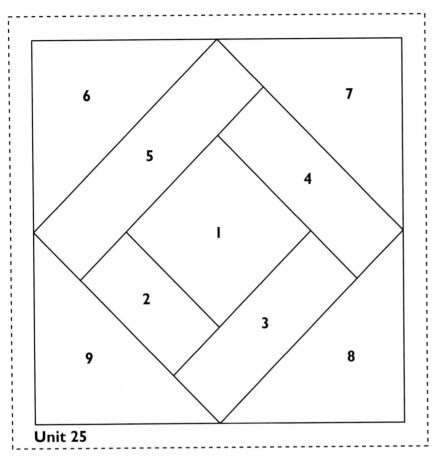

Unit 25

Unit 25

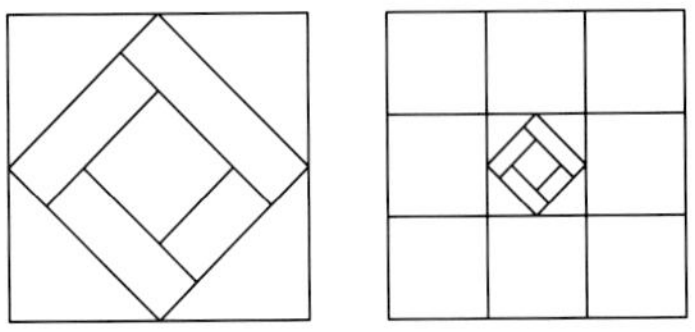

Cutting List for Unit 25

Location	Size to Cut	1 Unit
1	2" x 2"	1
2	1½" x 2"	1
3, 4	1½" x 2¾"	2
5	1½" x 3½"	1
6, 7, 8, 9	3¼" x 3¼" ◻	2

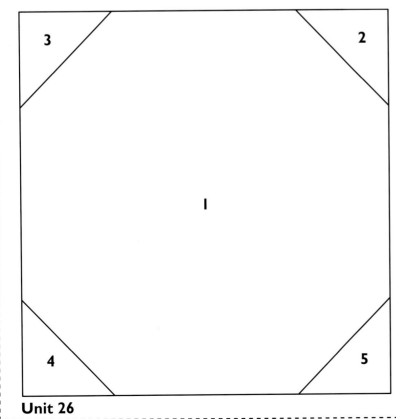

Unit 26

Unit 26

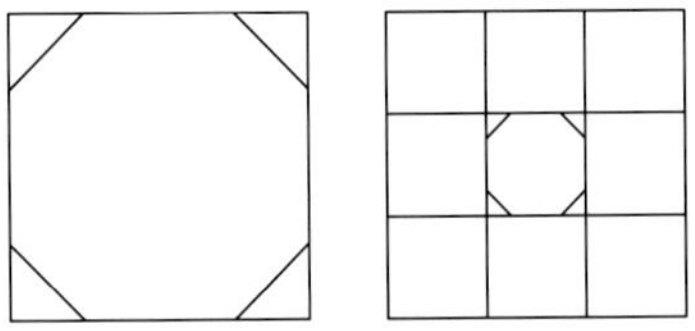

Cutting List for Unit 26

Location	Size to Cut	1 Unit
1	4¾" x 4¾"	1
2, 3, 4, 5	2¼" x 2¼" ◻	2

Unit 27

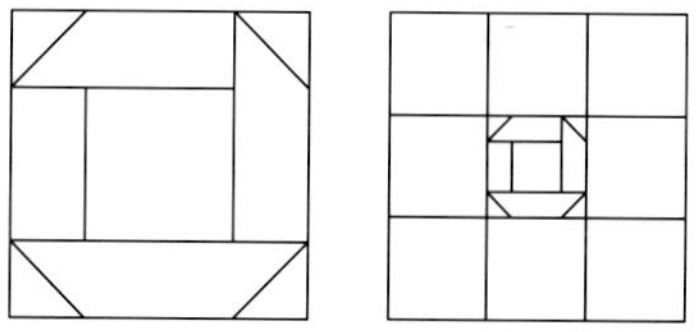

Cutting List for Unit 27

Location	Size to Cut	1 Unit
1	2¾" x 2¾"	1
2	1¾" x 2¾"	1
3, 4	1¾" x 3¾"	2
5	1¾" x 4¾"	1
6, 7, 8, 9	2¼" x 2¼" �	2

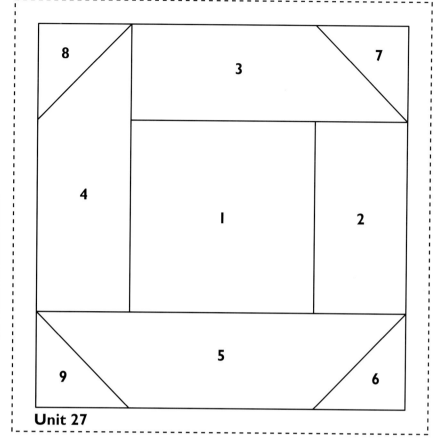

Unit 27

Unit 28

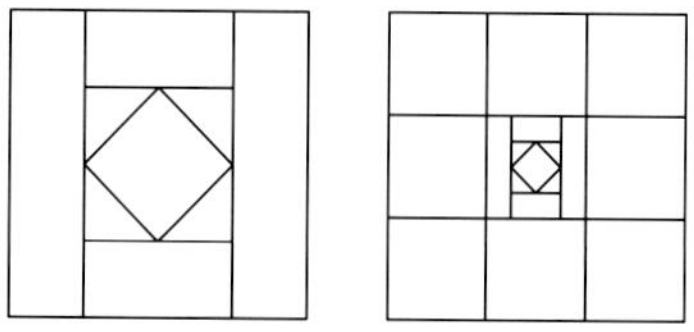

Cutting List for Unit 28

Location	Size to Cut	1 Unit
1	2" x 2"	1
2, 3, 4, 5	2¼" x 2¼" ◻	2
6, 7	1¾" x 2¾"	2
8, 9	1¾" x 4¾"	2

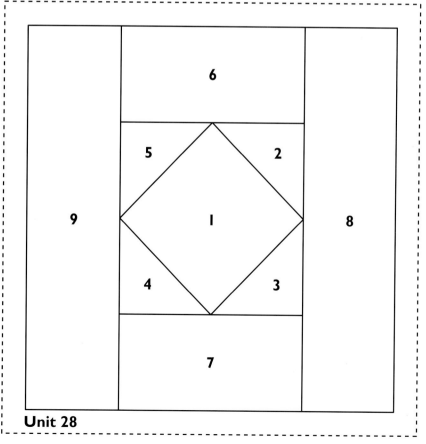

Unit 28

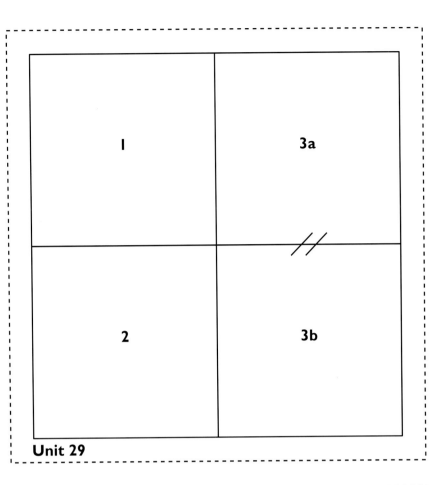

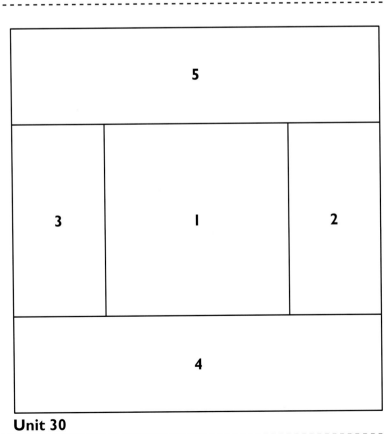

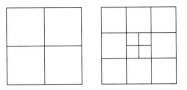

Unit 29

Cutting List for Unit 29

Location	Size to Cut	1 Unit
1, 2, 3a, 3b*	2¾" x 2¾"	4

*For a strip piece option, see page 23.

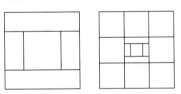

Unit 30

Cutting List for Unit 30

Location	Size to Cut	1 Unit
1	2¾" x 2¾"	1
2, 3	1¾" x 2¾"	2
4, 5	1¾" x 4¾"	2

Corner Units

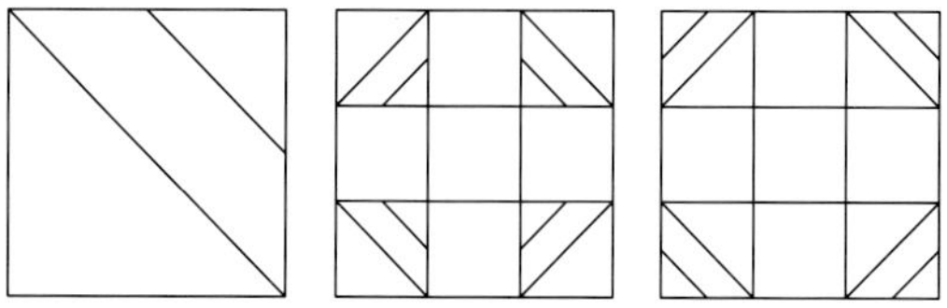

Unit 31

Cutting List for Unit 31

Location	Size to Cut	4 Units
1	5¼" x 5¼" ◿	2
2	2" x 6½"	4
3	3¼" x 3¼" ◿	2

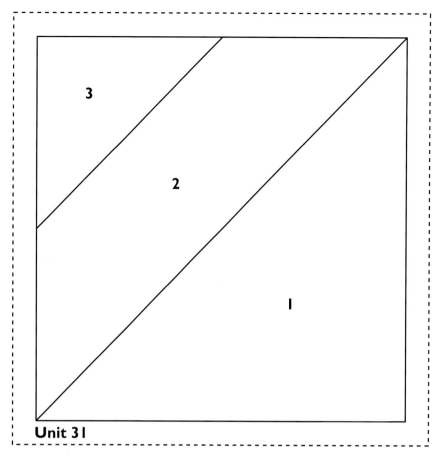

Unit 31

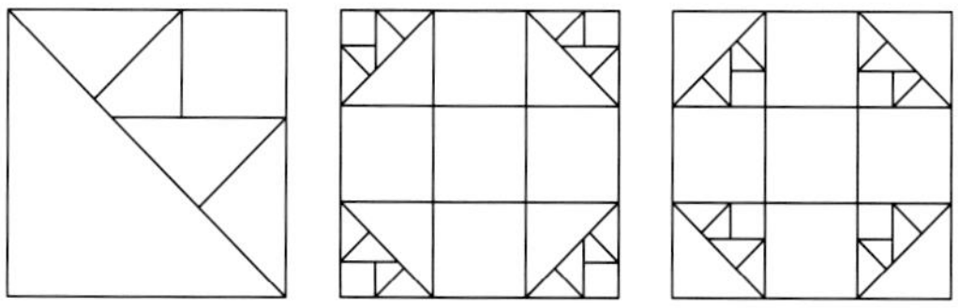

Unit 32

Cutting List for Unit 32

Location	Size to Cut	4 Units
1	2¼" x 2¼"	4
2	2¾" x 2¾" ◿	2
3, 4, 5	4" x 4" ⊠	3
6	5¼" x 5¼" ◿	2

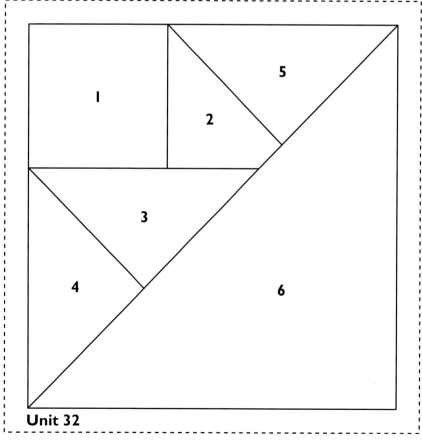

Unit 32

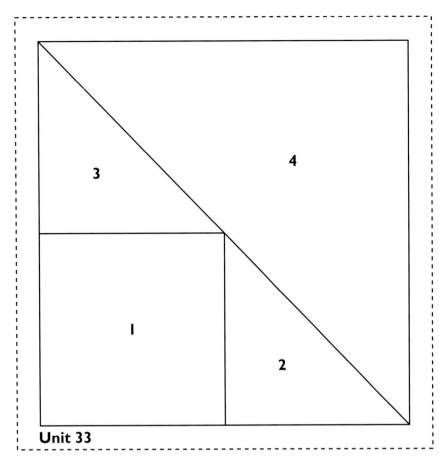

Unit 33

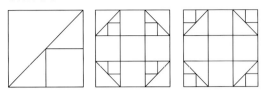

Cutting List for Unit 33

Location	Size to Cut	4 Units
1	2¾" x 2¾"	4
2, 3	3¼" x 3¼" ◻	4
4	5¼" x 5¼" ◻	2

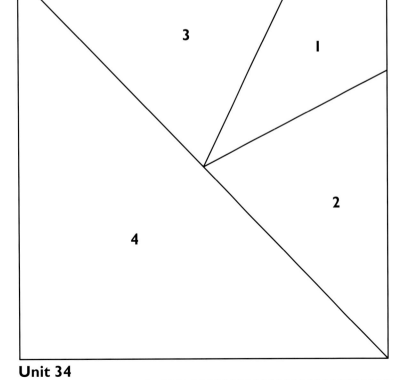

Unit 34

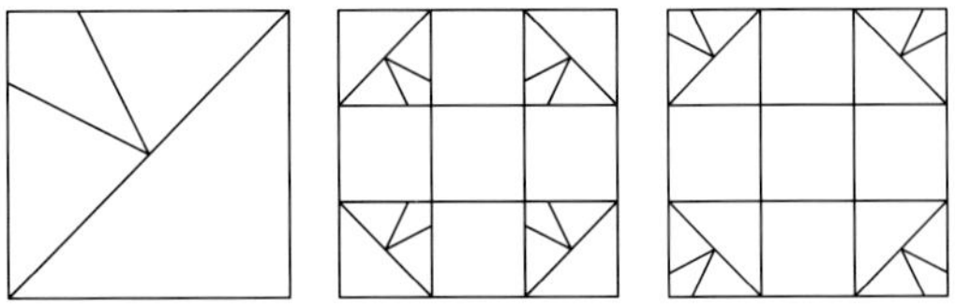

Cutting List for Unit 34

Location	Size to Cut	4 Units
1	2" x 3½"	4
2, 3	3¼" x 3¼"	8
4	5¼" x 5¼" ◻	2

Unit 35

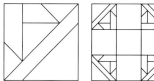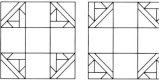

Cutting List for Unit 35

Location	Size to Cut	4 Units
1	3¼″ x 3¼″ ◹	2
2	1¾″ x 2¾″	4
3	1¾″ x 3¾″	4
4, 5	3½″ x 3½″ ⊠	2
6	1¼″ x 6½″	4
7	4¼″ x 4¼″ ◹	2

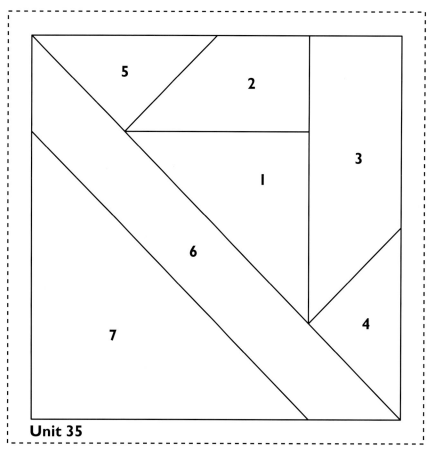

Unit 35

Unit 36

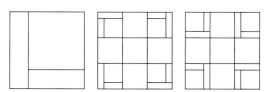

Cutting List for Unit 36

Location	Size to Cut	4 Units
1	3¾″ x 3¾″	4
2	1¾″ x 3¾″	4
3	1¾″ x 4¾″	4

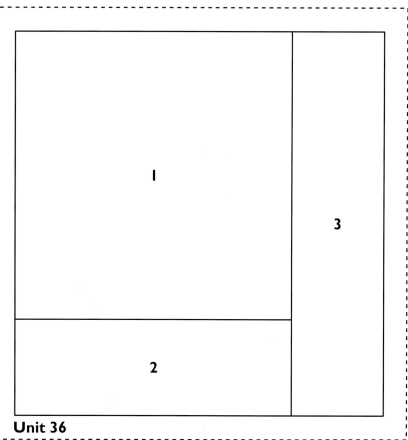

Unit 36

Unit 37

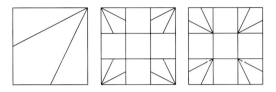

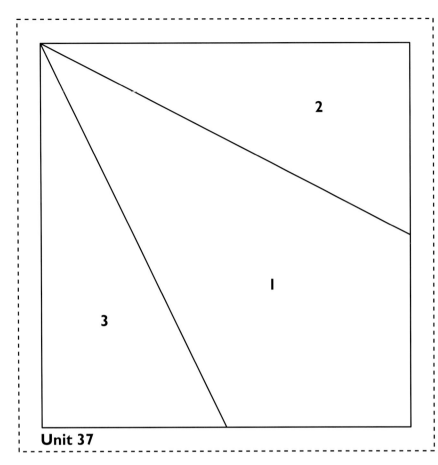

Unit 37

Cutting List for Unit 37

Location	Size to Cut	4 Units
1	3½" x 6½"	4
2, 3	2½" x 5½"	8

Unit 38

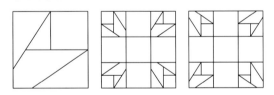

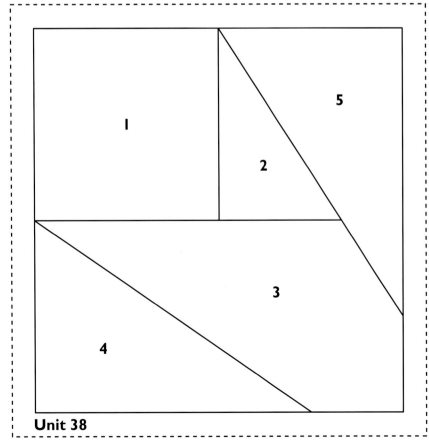

Unit 38

Cutting List for Unit 38

Location	Size to Cut	4 Units
1	2¾" x 2¾"	4
2	2" x 2¾"	4
3	2¾" x 4¾"	4
4, 5	2¼" x 4½"	8

Unit 39

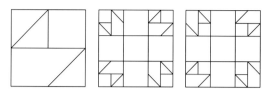

Cutting List for Unit 39

Location	Size to Cut	4 Units
1	2¾" x 2¾"	4
2, 4, 5	3¼" x 3¼" ▱	6
3	2¾" x 4¾"	4

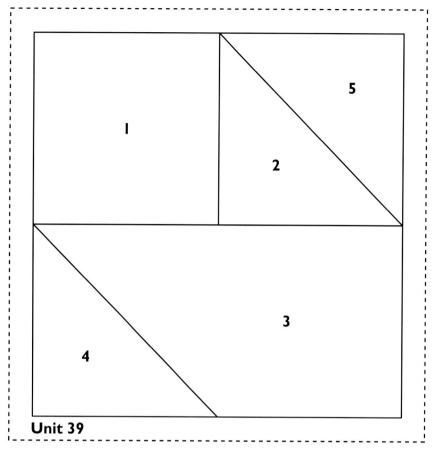

Unit 39

Unit 40

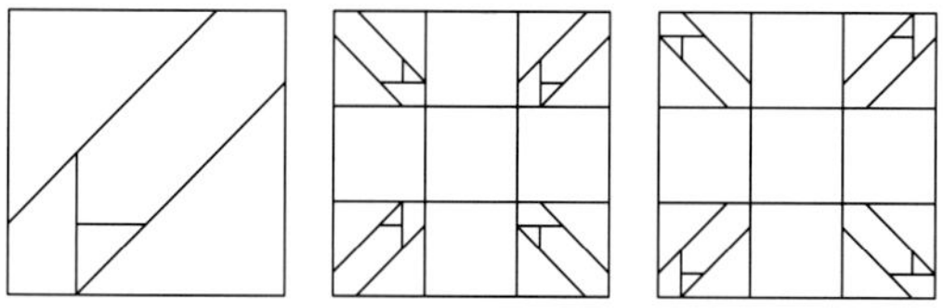

Cutting List for Unit 40

Location	Size to Cut	4 Units
1	2" x 5"	4
2	2¼" x 2¼" ▱	2
3	1¾" x 2¾"	4
4, 5	4¼" x 4¼" ▱	4

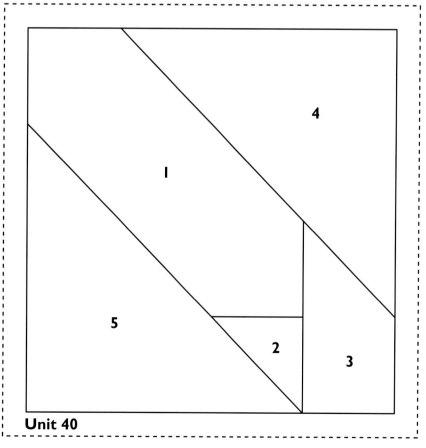

Unit 40

Resources

Carol Doak's Foundation Paper

C&T Publishing, Inc.
800-284-1114
www.ctpub.com

Add-A-Quarter Ruler

CM Designs
7968 Kelty Trail
Franktown, CO 80116
303-841-5920

Curved Pointed Snips

Tool-Tron Industries
830-249-8277
tooltron@texas.net

Carol Doak newsletter and web page

http://quilt.com/CDoak

For more information ask for a free catalog:
C&T Publishing, Inc.
P.O. Box 1456
Lafayette, CA 94549
800-284-1114
ctinfo@ctpub.com
www.ctpub.com

For quilting supplies:
Cotton Patch Mail Order
3405 Hall Lane, Dept. CTB
Lafayette, CA 94549
800-835-4418
quiltusa@yahoo.com
www.quiltusa.com

Note: Fabrics used in the quilts shown may not be currently available since fabric manufacturers keep most fabrics in print for only a short time.

Foundation Factory CD to print the foundations

Quilt-Pro Systems, Inc.
P.O. Box 560692
The Colony, TX 75056
800-884-1511

System requirements:

PC system requirements: Windows 95/98/NT4/2000/ME/XP, 8MB RAM, 20MB hard disk space, mouse or compatible pointing device

Mac system requirements: Power Macintosh system running Mac OS X or higher, 16MB RAM, 20MB hard disk space, mouse or compatible pointing device

PC installation:

1. Insert the CD into your CD drive.

2. The system should automatically run the installation. If it doesn't, click on the Start button and select Run. Enter D:\setup (where D is your CD-ROM drive) and press Enter or click the OK button.

3. Follow the on-screen instructions.

Mac installation:

1. Insert the CD into your CD drive.

2. A window should open. If not, double click on the CD icon to open the window. In the window, double-click on the Foundation Factory Installer.

3. Follow the on-screen instructions.

For help with installation or running the program, call 972-625-0819 or email techsupport@quiltpro.com.

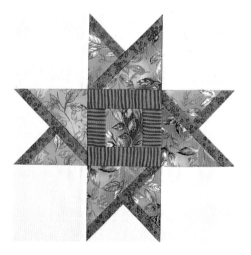

About the Author

Carol Doak's passion for quiltmaking began in 1979 when she enrolled in a basic quilting class in Worthington, Ohio. She taught that class the following year and continues to share her passion with quilters worldwide through her sizable collection of best-selling books and popular classes. Her teaching style has been described as lighthearted and fun, with the goal of inspiring students in a positive way.

In 1994, her first paper-piecing book, *Easy Machine Paper Piecing*, popularized her trademark technique worldwide. Carol's impressive quilts have been featured on the covers of most national quilting magazines. She writes a "Paper Piecing Possibilities" column for *The Quilter Magazine*.

In April 1999, Carol was awarded the 8th Honors Award from the East Coast Quilters Alliance in recognition of her outstanding influence in the field of quilting. In September 1999, *Easy Machine Paper Piecing* was named by *Quilter's Newsletter Magazine* as one of the 30 most influential quilting books of the previous 30 years. Carol has been named one of the top ten quilt teachers and designers in the United States, and in 2004 she was nominated as one of 24 All-American Quilters. Carol resides in Windham, New Hampshire, with her husband.

Carol Doak's Foundation Paper

100 SHEETS

- Use in most inkjet or laser printers or copy machines

- No shrinking, curling, or turning brittle!

- Holds up beautifully during stitching; tears away easily when you're done

What makes Carol Doak's Foundation Paper *different?*

- **It's lightweight**
  -won't create bulk when you join sections
- **It's absorbent**
  -less ink transfer where you don't want it
- **It's non-coated**
  -fabric won't slip on it

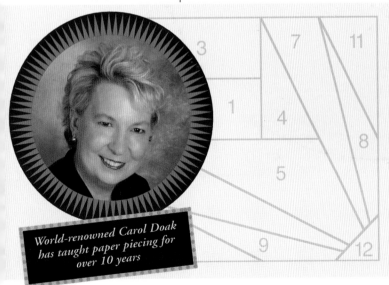

World-renowned Carol Doak has taught paper piecing for over 10 years

Discover Easy Paper Piecing with Carol Doak's Foundation Paper!

Tips for Easy Use

When using a photocopier, inkjet, or laser printer:
Fill paper tray with Carol Doak's Foundation Paper and print or copy your pattern. You may also hand-feed single sheets.

When tracing:
Lay a sheet of Carol Doak's Foundation Paper over pattern in book or magazine and place both over a light source. Trace with a fine-point permanent marker. A photocopy of the pattern is easier to handle than the actual book or magazine—just make sure the copy is exactly the same size as the pattern.

Pressing:
Use a dry iron on a cotton setting and a pressing cloth on your ironing board cover to protect it from excess ink.

Carol Doak
With 24 years of experience as a quilt teacher, Carol Doak has focused on paper piecing for the past decade. The popular designer and author also creates fabric collections for Timeless Treasures.

100 sheets, 8½" x 11"

C&T PUBLISHING

www.ctpub.com

UPC
$8.50
50850

7 34817 10985 3